BREXIT EXPOSED

The Brexit Chronicles

Lest we forget!

PAUL McQUEEN

Published by

Graystone LA

Tanner Business Centre

Chew Valley Road

Oldham OL3 7NH

United Kingdom

www.brexitchronicles.co.uk

Third Edition (revised)

A catalogue record for this book is available from the British Library

Copyright © Paul McQueen 2022

PREFACE

Brexit Exposed, chronicles the most important chain of events in British history since World War II. With tales of treachery and skulduggery, your view of the EU will never be the same.

After two failed attempts, Britain is eventually allowed to join the Common Market (EEC). This is 16 years after the six founding members have already signed the 'Treaty of Rome' which established the ground rules.

The 'six' have also written the rules for subsequent membership, knowing full well they don't entirely work in Britain's favour. In fact, the terms by which Britain signs up are so bad, that every single British prime minister without exception pushes hard for reforms, with only Margaret Thatcher ever achieving a success.

During the 47 years of membership, the British Parliament sign off treaty after EU treaty leading toward an ever closer union without once offering the people a say, in the form of a referendum. The two most significant EU treaties giving away British sovereignty are signed off by prime ministers who weren't elected to their post by the people – 'Maastricht Treaty' (John Major) and the 'Lisbon Treaty' (Gordon Brown).

Brexit Exposed simply tells it as it happened, following a timeline over 62 years, it gives you the clearest insight as to why Brexit was inevitable and the only option left.

In remembrance of
Her Majesty Queen Elizabeth II

~ 21 April 1926 to 8 September 2022

Her late Majesty served the nation for over 70 years, committed to the role of the constitutional Head of State with a strong sense of duty and determination. Her dignified leadership was an example to us all.

Politically neutral serving as a sounding board, she was privy to all matters of Government and a safeguard for parliamentary democracy through her weekly Audience with every standing prime minister. There were 15 leaders in all who served under her from Winston Churchill to Liz Truss.

The Queen helped shape British history, playing a crucial roll in securing the 2016 referendum, bringing a House of Commons defiant of their voters back in line.

Her Late Majesty was the one constant throughout.

Thank you Ma'am for your service.

Hotlifestyle
Sleep Strategies

For a Good Night's Sleep Every Night.

Getting a restful night's sleep is easier than you think with proven strategies to break you out of the cycle of tiredness. Establish healthy sleep patterns in record time forming good habits, avoiding the things that hinder a good night's sleep.

www.Hotlifestyle.info/sleep

Hotlifestyle - Fit for Fun

The Essential Basics for Living a Better Life

Create a competitive edge in your life with effective routines, making better choices. This is the only book to cover all the bases leading to a healthier happier richer you. Includes a free healthy shopping guide.

www.Hotlifestyle.info/F4F

18 THINGS THIS BOOK COVERS

- ➤ With the cards stacked in favour of Remain, why did they fail?

- ➤ A timeline of key-events joining the dots leading up to Brexit.

- ➤ The Queen's crucial role in securing the 2016 referendum.

- ➤ The real reason Margaret Thatcher was ousted from her Party.

- ➤ Find out what the EU is about and who it benefits most.

- ➤ On six occasions Brexit could've been thwarted, why wasn't it?

- ➤ Discover the ‚CAP' and how it cost Britain billions of pounds.

- ➤ How much influence does Germany really have over the EU?

- ➤ Why every single British prime minister pushed for EU reform.

- ➤ How informed were the public before the 2016 referendum?

- ➤ Britain was the second country to vote Leave. Who was first?

- ➤ Understand why MPs really didn't want a second referendum.

- ➤ Find out why a planned UK referendum had to be cancelled.

- ➤ What's the difference between democracy and EU democracy?

- ➤ Who said, 'there is a tradition of not holding referendums'?

- ➤ Major policy changes over 47 years. How many referendums?

- ➤ Cameron's defining moment, beginning seven years of hell.

- ➤ How much extra did the UK actually pay the EU in 2018?

TIMELINE

When it comes to Brexit,
nobody is impartial.

~ Paul McQueen

INTRODUCTION

Simply mentioning the 'B' word still provokes an extreme emotional response in everyone I talk to. Everybody has an opinion on the subject, to the point that they are simply compelled (obsessed) to share it with me. It has polarized a nation, to the extent that it seems every facet of life is now seen in terms of Leave or Remain. Political parties, newspapers, television programmes are all one side or the other. Unbiased media is a thing of the past. The 2016 referendum has torn apart families and friends, and tormented some to the point of murder (MP Jo Cox). Brits, famous for calm, stiff upper lips, and tolerance have become a nation of ranting protesting revolutionaries with an 'if you're not with us, then you're against us' attitude. Like two tribes going to war, any amount of treachery and skulduggery is acceptable, as long as it helps to win. Whatever happened to that sense of fairness, correctness, and justice that, in my opinion, separated us Brits from every other nation? Have these values simply fallen by the wayside?

So, on 23 June 2016, it happened. It was reported that Boris Johnson went to bed the previous evening resolved that he had done his best but was defeated. After all, our leaders and the polls were very clear, the Remain vote would win by a safe margin. But, much to the surprise of those who were campaigning for Brexit, they actually won.

The next day, after learning of the result, I had this crazy notion, Leave meant Leave, and that MPs would suppress their own bias to pursue the will of the people. After all, this is not Somalia or Mexico we're talking about, this is Britain for god's sake! You'd think that our elected lawmakers should be able to step up to the mark. This was sadly not the case as each MP jockeyed for position to pursue their own Brexit leaning.

At the time of the 2016 referendum, 80% of MPs on both sides of the House are for Remain. This creates a huge dilemma. Consider that 70% of people in Labour constituencies voted for Brexit, then Labour leader Jeremy Corbyn announces, 'Labour will become the Remain Party'. You can see the problem.

Watching Cllr Luisa Porritt MEP (Lib-Dems) holding a 'Stop Brexit' banner and spouting how Boris Johnson is flouting democracy, demonstrates the hypocrisy of elected politicians who showed little respect for a decision made by the people.

I have always been interested to know what motivates people to behave in a certain way. What makes people tick? Why do some find life hard and others seem to glide through it with ease? Why do some people make bad choices at times when they should go far? Why do people shoot themselves in the foot? To this end I began a series of books around lifestyle choices. Writing the Hotlifestyle series made me ask, why would 21 Members of Parliament choose to vote against their own party and moreover against their constituents, knowing full well that the consequences would be dismissal. Long-serving MPs who have enjoyed top positions in their party chose to throw their career away because of Brexit.

Was there so much conflict in the mind of MP Jo Johnson (brother of Boris), that he saw no other alternative but to quit politics altogether?

Never have we seen people so emotionally charged about a subject that they behave irrationally, so great is their pain and so deep is their passion. It seems that when it comes to Brexit, nobody is impartial.

Immediately after the referendum, the Remainers took control of the narrative, feeling cheated as the clear outcome promised by the politicians failed to materialize. The media play their part in fuelling the conflict as it makes a great story which helps sell more newspapers.

The acts of treachery and skulduggery by the media and our lawmakers post-referendum, made a laughing stock of the UK around the world. They have dumped on the very principles that made this country great.

This seems to be their plan after the Referendum

Drag out and frustrate the Brexit process to a point where the general public will agree to anything just to make it go away.

The Brexit saga was 62 years in the making

The Brexit story began long before the 2016 referendum. An in-out referendum was on the table just two years after Britain joined the then 'Common Market' in 1973. The 1975 in-out referendum went in favour of Remain and, although the result was different to 2016, there are striking similarities between the actions of PM Harold Wilson and David Cameron's more recent tactics. Comparisons can also be drawn with Britain's fundamental ,problems' with European integration.

This book is about those people in power whose wholehearted belief in a vision of a United States of Europe experienced a massive setback. It's about the leaders who set a course to unification but failing to involve the general public in the decision-making process. It's about a public who are just as divided on Europe today as they were back in 1975.

Let me walk you down the corridors of power as the plot to bring a mostly unwilling nation into the EU-fold gathers momentum, only to fail through a referendum 43 years on.

The Brexit saga has never before been compiled chronologically, giving the clearest insight into what really happened and why. You are in for some big surprises!

I'll highlight events and key players who helped form the opinions of a nation. I'll name names, quoting from those in power to reveal who told the truth, who prophesied the end game and who simply made an ass of themselves.

I'm very concerned by the way our view of current affairs is distorted by a mainstream media that relies so heavily on speculation. Perhaps we should redefine the word 'news' since today it is made up of 10% fact and 90% speculation.

THE BOTTOM LINE

Speculation is not news.

Let's take a look at the facts and the opinion makers who led Britain down a path of ever closer EU union. Let's expose the broken promises, deceit, and hypocrisy from all those who, too often, omitted the pieces of information that didn't suit their own bias.

The bigger picture why Brexit was inevitable can only be seen when looking back over 62 years from the inception of the Common Market to David Cameron's speech 3 January 2013 announcing the referendum which created seven years of hell 'til Britain finally left the EU on 31 January 2020.

Whether you're in the 'Remain' or the 'Leave' camp, reading the Brexit Exposed, the Brexit Chronicles will give you a truly informed view of why we are where we are today. This is an honest catalogue of Britain's path to leaving the EU.

Having a grasp of how EU power is constructed through its institutions, will help you understand who has control and how this influences relations between member states.

Let's take a look at three EU institutions

It's important from the onset to have a basic understanding of the workings of the three main institutions (there are seven in total) that drive the EU:

➤ The European Commission

➤ The European Council

➤ The European Parliament

Each body operates independently and has a President. These Presidents are the main players in driving and controlling EU policy.

The European Commission (EC)

The European Commission is made up of one representative from each member state, usually an ex-high-ranking politician. The commissioners are responsible for drafting laws and treaties and can propose new legislation. They ensure that EU laws and treaties are obeyed, which is why the Commission is also known as the Guardian of the Treaties.

Past EC Presidents you might recognize are José Manuel Barroso (EPP) (2004-2014), Jean-Claude Juncker (EPP) (2014-2019) and Ursula von der Leyen (EPP) (2019-2024). (EPP - The 'European People's Party' is the largest political group of MEPs within the European Parliament.) The 'EC' is by far the most powerful of the three institutions, which is why it's important to have the right person as President. The Treaty of

Lisbon states that Presidents are chosen by the Council and then presented to the European Parliament for approval.

The European Council (EUCO)

Members of this exclusive club are current heads of state or government of the EU member states. They are often seen sitting at a large round table at summits, where they agree the EU's overall political direction and priorities. The EC President also sits at the table with the EUCO President.

EUCO Presidents have been ex-politicians, like Herman Van Rompuy (EPP) (2009-2014), Donald Tusk (EPP) (2014-2019), Charles Michel (ALDE) (1 December 2019 - 31 May 2022).

The European Parliament (EP)

The European Parliament is currently made up of 751 Members of the European Parliament (MEPs), voted in by 400 million people in elections held every five years. It is the only EU institution that is directly elected, but no legislation is made in the EP. The EP President is elected by the MEPs and a term lasts 2.5 years. They chair debates and oversee all the activities of the Parliament. It is mainly an administrative role but holds a similar position to that of Speaker in the House of Commons.

Presidents are usually politicians who became MEPs, Hans-Gert Pöttering (2007-2009), Antonio Tajani (2017-2019) and David-Maria Sassoli (S&D) (July 2019 - December 2021).

BOOK ONE

THE COMMON MARKET YEARS

(1958 - 1992)

INTRODUCTION

Tales of Treachery and Skulduggery

One of the most important aspects to consider in this era is, why didn't Britain sign the 1957 Treaty of Rome (along with the six original members - France, West Germany, Belgium, Italy, Luxembourg, and the Netherlands) that created the European Economic Community (EEC / Common Market)?

In hindsight it's easy to criticize, but had Britain been instrumental in the formation of EEC policies from the very beginning it would have had more say in the make-up of the treaty. Especially with regard to the **Common Agricultural Policy (CAP)**, which is written in favour of France.

As Sir Geoffrey Howe (Con) pointed out in his resignation speech November 1990, „If we had been in from the start, we should have had more, not less, influence over the Europe in which we live today."

It was the supranational nature of the Treaty of Rome that made Britain pull out of negotiations early on. So it is Britain's choice not to participate in the talks leading up to the signing of the Treaty of Rome. And not for the first time.

During negotiations back in 1951 between France and Germany on the European Coal and Steel Community (predecessor to the Treaty of Rome), Britain also withdrew from talks when the supranational nature of the treaty was defined.

It must be taken into consideration that in the 1950s, Britain is a global economic powerhouse in its own right through established trading channels with its colonies and the British Commonwealth (Canada, Australia, New Zealand, South Africa, India, Pakistan, Sri Lanka, Irish Free State, and Newfoundland). It also enjoys a special relationship with the United States.

Britain has its own agenda for pursuing a 'one-world economic system' policy with the pound sterling as the central currency, English as the language, and Britain at the centre of a flourishing Commonwealth.

The British government believes in tariff-free trade. If tariffs are to be applied, then each country should decide independently with whom and by how much – in contrast to the policies of the EEC, with its centralized system for tariffs run from Brussels. This means the EEC dictating the tariffs Britain should charge on Commonwealth imports, if they join.

The Commonwealth grew out of a British Empire that held sway over a quarter of the world's population by 1922 (about 458 million people). It grew significantly throughout the 1970s and can boast a total of 53 countries today.

The Late Queen was head of the Commonwealth and as such her image appeared on money and stamps in many Commonwealth countries with English being widely spoken.

In the 1950s Europe, still recovering economically from World War II, has very little to offer in the way of trade with Britain, who is putting its future into building up the Commonwealth.

In a famous post-war speech 1946, Winston Churchill says: 'The position of Britain is to support European integration, especially between Germany and France, since it is a solid way to avoid future wars on the continent.'

Churchill later commented,

> *'Britain should have been a friend of*
> *European integration, but never a part of it.'*

During the 1950s, France and Germany are the dominant force in Europe and experience rapid recovery after World War II, partly due to the implementation of the Marshall Plan. The Marshall Plan, a US initiative started in 1948, saw the US donate over $12 billion (the equivalent of nearly $100 billion in 2020 terms) in aid to help rebuild war-torn economies. The largest recipient of aid by far was the United Kingdom (about 26% of the total), followed by France (18%), and West Germany (11%). The rest went to 18 other European countries involved in World War II.

After refusing to sign up to the EEC in 1957, the British then opt for a new organization based on a free trade area without any form of supranational ambition. In January 1960 the Treaty of Stockholm is signed, and the European Free Trade Association (EFTA) is founded, creating a free trade area for industrial goods. Party to the treaty are: Great Britain, Denmark, Sweden, Norway, Portugal, Austria, Ireland, and Switzerland.

Move on a year to 1961 and we see a world that has significantly changed. Mainland Europe is growing faster than Britain and the government of the day fears diplomatic and economic exclusion from Europe. To the British Government it now looks like joining the EEC could have significant benefits.

Only on the third attempt is Britain able to join the EEC. It has no influence on policy as the Treaty of Rome is already established and the 'six' founding members will not adapt it to appease those now wanting to be part of their club. Any new member has to accept all EEC communitarian policies, and not just some.

It's a bad deal for Britain right from the start as signatories fail to assess the financial damage that the 'CAP' will inflict.

Eleven years later Margaret Thatcher remedies this unfair practice to some extent, negotiating a 66% rebate; only for the benefits to be given away by Tony Blair who thought it would help him to become the first EU President.

> ## The Brexit saga begins with the signing of the Treaty of Rome

CHAPTER ONE

Walking the Dinosaur

March 1957 - Signing the Treaty of Rome

The signing of the Treaty of Rome by six member states (France, West Germany, Belgium, Italy, Luxembourg, and the Netherlands) creates the European Economic Community (EEC) - or the Common Market as it is referred to in Britain.

The treaty comes into force on 1 January 1958. It seeks to reduce customs duties, create a **Common Agricultural Policy** (CAP), a common transport policy, and a European social fund among member states. It is without question one of the most important treaties ever to be drafted and implemented anywhere in the world – and the 'CAP' is central to it.

The CAP - from a British perspective

Farming is a challenging business that depends on many factors for success, including weather, climate, supply and demand, and pest control. France has 20% of its workforce engaged in farming and pushes early on for policies that promote the interests of their farming industry.

The French government, led by Charles de Gaulle (1959–1969), is supported heavily by French farmers, which means keeping them happy to remain in power, which means keeping food prices artificially high. France's agricultural sector is five times bigger than Britain's, so a Common Agricultural Policy (CAP) is an important factor in any treaty France signs up to.

Only general principles for a CAP are approved in the Treaty of Rome. Details are delayed by many years, until de Gaulle's lobbying, forces other members to sign up to it. De Gaulle doesn't want the UK to join the EEC until the CAP is approved by the six founding members. He knows the British will want to limit the detrimental consequences of this policy as it does not work in Britain's interests.

The CAP is based on enforcing fair food prices (for farmers), together with tariffs on imported foods from non-ECC countries, to ensure there's no undercutting of prices.

Britain, with its relatively small farming sector, is heavily reliant on cheap food imports from the Commonwealth and other countries.

British farmers are also subsidised by the tax payer as part of a British cheap food trade policy.

Not one of the original six EEC members has anything like the benefits that Britain enjoys through association with the Commonwealth.

There are two main CAP principles:

1. All EEC members should be treated equally - meaning Britain cannot be given preferential treatment by allowing tariff-free imports from outside the EEC.

2. EEC members should be treated better than non-EEC members - meaning only food bought from within the EEC can be tariff free.

THE BOTTOM LINE

A Clash of Policies

The Common Agricultural Policy ensures higher prices for the consumer and subsidies to farmers paid for by the duties imposed on imports from non-EEC countries.

The British policy of tariff-free imports from the Commonwealth and subsidies to British farmers creates the cheap food trade policy.

These opposing policies are not compatible with one another and the six EEC members refuse to compromise during negotiations. They say it is up to Britain to adopt all the policies of the EEC if they want to join. This means that Britain will be forced to impose duty tariffs on all imports coming from Commonwealth countries.

The six founding members of the EEC cannot allow a new member preferential treatment over suppliers from within the EEC. In real terms this means a rise in the cost of living ending the cheap food policy, buying more expensive food from Europe, and taxing non-EEC imports so as not to undermine European farmers.

Even with a levy on imports from the Commonwealth, France still believes there will be an incentive for Britain to bring in food from outside the EEC, benefiting from import duties. So, during Britain's initial negotiations, the six members create a new budgetary policy in reply to: 'What was to happen with monies collected through import duties?' The answer is simple.

Send money collected via import duties to Brussels

The original six EEC members decide that all import taxes will be sent to the European Agricultural Guidance and Guarantee Fund (EAGGF), set up in 1962 in Brussels. The fund will distribute the money to member states, in proportion to the size of their agricultural sector.

Who benefits the most from this arrangement?

The country with the largest agriculture sector, namely France. Any other subsidising of farmers by individual countries is not allowed.

This means that due to Britain's small agricultural sector and food imports from Commonwealth countries, it will be paying the most in but getting the least out, making Britain the second largest contributor to the fund within two years of joining. French farmers benefiting from large subsidies due to British taxes paid directly into Brussels allow rapid modernization of the farming sector to take place. Meanwhile, British farmers have their subsidies cut, stifling growth, and putting an end to the cheap food trade policy.

The British rebate demanded by PM Margaret Thatcher in June 1984 is an attempt to remedy this unfair practice.

October 1959 - Conservative Party wins election

The third consecutive victory for the Conservative Party, now led by Prime Minister Harold Macmillan (1957–1963). Boosted by strong economic growth, the election is fought on the slogan 'You've never had it so good'. Britain is faring well just 14 years after the end of World War II.

Margaret Thatcher (Con) is elected MP for Finchley and takes her seat in the House of Commons for the first time.

May 1960 - The trade bloc EFTA is established

Iceland, Liechtenstein, Norway, and Switzerland create the European Free Trade Association (EFTA) as an alternative trade bloc for those unable, or unwilling, to join the EEC. The Stockholm Convention (EFTA Treaty) is signed on 4 January 1960 by seven countries, including Britain.

July 1961 - Negotiations begin to join the EEC

The United Kingdom, Ireland, and Denmark open negotiations to join the EEC. The British Conservative Prime Minister, Harold Macmillan, is watching the EEC very closely as growth in Europe exceeds that in Britain. He's worried about being excluded and wants to be part of a now booming Europe.

January 1963 - Britain's first application vetoed

Britain's first attempt to join the EEC is thwarted by French President Charles De Gaulle, who fears that it could open the door to unwanted influence from America.

He views Britain's membership of the EEC as potentially destabilizing, fearing that Britain's presence would weaken France's influence within the EEC with the British wanting to 'impose its own conditions'.

In an interview, De Gaulle justifies blocking Britain's entry citing that France looks forward to being the dominant force within the EEC.

Question: 'Could you define explicitly France's position towards Britain's entry into the Common Market and the political evolution of Europe?'

De Gaulle: 'In this very great affair of the European Economic Community and also in that of eventual adhesion of Great Britain, it is the facts that must first be considered.'

'The Treaty of Rome was concluded between six continental States. States which are, economically speaking, one may say, of the same nature. Indeed, whether it be a matter of their industrial or agricultural production, their external exchanges, their habits or their commercial clientele, their living or working conditions, there is between them much more resemblance than difference. Moreover, they are adjacent, they interpenetrate, they prolong each other through their communications. It is therefore a fact to group them and to link them in such a way that what they have to produce, to buy, to sell, to consume - well, they do produce, buy, sell, consume, in preference in their own ensemble. Doing that is conforming to realities.'

'When the Treaty of Rome was signed in 1957, it was after long discussions; and when it was concluded, it was necessary - in order to achieve something - that we French put in order our economic, financial, and monetary affairs ... and that was done in 1959.'

'However, this treaty, which was precise and complete enough concerning industry, was not at all so on the subject of agriculture. However, for our country this had to be settled. Indeed, it is obvious that agriculture is an essential element in the whole of our national activity. We cannot conceive, and will not conceive, of a Common Market in which French agriculture would not find outlets in keeping with its production. And we agree, further, that of the ‚six' we are the country on which this necessity is imposed in the most imperative manner.'

General de Gaulle was afraid that Britain might jeopardise the Common Agricultural Policy (CAP) and transform the European Economic Community (EEC) into a huge free trade area. Charles De Gaulle went on to say:

'England in effect is insular, she is maritime, she is linked through her exchanges, her markets, her supply lines to the most diverse and often the most distant countries; she pursues essentially industrial and commercial activities, and only slight agricultural ones. She has in all her doings very marked and very original habits and traditions. In short, the nature, the structure, the very situation (conjuncture) that are England's differ profoundly from those of the continentals.'

'What is to be done in order that England, as she lives, produces and trades, can be incorporated into the Common Market, as it has been conceived and as it functions? For example, the means by which the people of Great Britain are fed and which are in fact the importation of foodstuffs bought cheaply in the two Americas and in the former dominions, at the same time giving, granting considerable subsidies to

English farmers? These means are obviously incompatible with the system which the ‚six' have established quite naturally for themselves.'

'The system of the ‚six' - this constitutes making a whole of the agricultural produce of the whole Community, in strictly fixing their prices, in prohibiting subsidies, in organising their consumption between all the participants, and in imposing on each of its participants payment to the Community of any saving they would achieve in fetching their food from outside instead of eating what the EEC has to offer. Once again, what is to be done to bring England, as she is, into this system?'

'One might sometimes have believed that our English friends, in posing their candidature to the Common Market, were agreeing to transform themselves to the point of applying all the conditions which are accepted and practised by the 'six'. But the question, to know whether Great Britain can now place herself like the Continent and with it inside a tariff which is genuinely common, to renounce all Commonwealth preferences, to cease any pretence that her agriculture be privileged, and, more than that, to treat her engagements with other countries of the free trade area as null and void — that question is the whole question.'

Upon hearing the news Prime Minister Macmillan wrote in his diary: "The French always betray you in the end."

At this point in time, the Common Agricultural Policy (CAP) was not yet ratified by the EEC.

October 1963 - Macmillan resigns as Prime Minister

Macmillan uses a terminal cancer diagnosis to immediately resign as Prime Minister and retires from politics. In September 1964 he takes up the chairmanship of his family's publishing business – Macmillan Publishers – lives a further 23 years and dies at the ripe old age of 92.

October 1964 - Labour narrowly win the election

The Labour Party beats the Conservatives by only four seats at the general election. Harold Wilson becomes prime minister (1964–1970 and again in 1974–1976). First on his agenda is dealing with an inherited deficit of £800 million.

March 1966 - Labour wins the election by a landslide

Labour Prime Minister Harold Wilson calls a snap election after only 17 months in government because of his meager four-seat majority. It pays off. He now commands a massive 98-seat majority in the House.

The Scottish National Party (SNP) win no seats in Parliament, despite putting 23 candidates forward.

March 1966 - Decimalization announced

Chancellor of the Exchequer James Callaghan announces to Parliament the intention to introduce decimalization. Although it has been discussed in Britain since 1847 the government decides to act fairly quickly after the election, aware that joining the Common Market will raise food prices due to CAP import duty policies.

The currency system of pounds, shillings, and pence, in which one pound is equal to 240 pennies, would be converted to one pound equalling 100 new pence.
The old pound note (a quid, written as £1) was worth 240 pennies. The ten-shilling note (or ten bob, written as 10s or 10/-) was worth 120 pennies and the shilling (a bob, written as 1s or 1/-) was worth 12 pennies (written as 12d).

The Decimal Currency Board (DCB) is created to manage the transition by 15 February 1971, called D-day.

Those who experienced the switch to decimal currency say things get more expensive. Inflation is about 9% when the new money is introduced and, despite everything, prices begin to soar after February 1971.

James Callaghan gives an enthusiastic interview to explain the benefits of decimalization. Its cost to industry is around £128 million and £23.5 million to the government − £1 million of that for advertising and publicity.

> **Was decimalization a ploy to confuse the public in anticipation of Common Market membership?**

November 1967 - Pound devalued on Black Monday

To address a mounting deficit, the Chancellor of the Exchequer James Callaghan reluctantly devalues sterling by 14% to make imports more expensive and exports cheaper. This causes inflation to rise.

November 1967 - Second attempt to join vetoed

Labour Prime Minister Harold Wilson's attempt to join the EEC is vetoed yet again by the President of France. Charles de Gaulle says that Britain harbours a 'deep-seated hostility' to any pan-European project and that 'Economy, working practices and agriculture made Britain incompatible with Europe'.

The other five members support Britain's entry but, are warned that if they try to impose British membership on France it would result in the break-up of the Community.

July 1969 - French President supports UK application

France has a new President. Georges Pompidou (1969–1974, elected on a pro-European manifesto) wants to enlarge EEC membership and his initiative is supported by all member states at the Hague EEC summit conference. Leaders agree to open negotiations with four applicant countries: Great Britain, Ireland, Denmark, and Norway.

The conclusion drawn by a British Cabinet discussion on 22 July 1969, provides an indication of the difficulties Britain will face negotiating entry:

'Should the French insist on the satisfaction of their agricultural demands (CAP) in full as a price for agreeing to negotiations for British entry, we should be in a difficult position. The price we should have to pay might be too high, and we should not seek membership of the EEC at any cost.'

Only after France ensures that other countries will subsidise her farming sector through the Common Agricultural Policy (CAP), do they actively pursue British entry.

Britain will be forced to impose duties on imports of food from the Commonwealth. The proceeds of those taxes will go directly to the EAGGF in Brussels to fund the CAP and French Farmers.

THE CRUX OF IT

Britain will be handing over money it collects in import duties to subsidise French farmers and simultaneously provide those farmers with a market for their goods.

June 1970 - Conservatives win a landslide election

The Conservative Party, led by Edward (Ted) Heath, surprisingly defeats the ruling Labour Party in a general election. They win 330 seats to 228, compared to the last election's 253 to 364 for Labour. A swing in the country's mood loses Labour, led by Harold Wilson, a massive 77 seats and ends 13 years of Labour rule.

The opinion polls have got it wrong, predicting a comfortable Labour victory with at least a 12% lead over the Conservatives. The polls completely underestimated how devaluing the pound, coupled with inflation and high interest rates, would damage Labour's credibility.

Ted Heath is a strong supporter of the EEC and sets out to negotiate Britain's entry. But his tenure is marked by major industrial strikes and high inflation.

CHAPTER TWO

Britain Joins the Common Market

January 1972 - Signing the Treaty of Accession

On the third attempt, and after years of negotiation, Britain joins the EEC without consulting the people. Ireland and Denmark join at the same time, but only after holding a referendum. Norway's referendum goes against joining. That's right, four countries are invited to join the EEC; three of them hold a referendum but Britain doesn't.

UK Prime Minister Edward Heath, leader of the Conservative Party (1970-1974), signs the Treaty of Accession in Brussels on 22 January 1972. It is to take effect on 1 January 1973.

So, here's a peculiarity of British politics.
First sign the treaty, then get parliamentary approval.

An Act of Parliament is required for the treaty to take effect as no referendum was held. So, just four days after Heath signs the treaty, the European Communities Act 1972 is being read in parliament.

January 1972 - The European Communities Act 1972

22 January 1972 - Treaty of Accession signed in Brussels.

26 January 1972 - Bill introduced to the House of Commons for the first time by MP Geoffrey Rippon.

17 February 1972 - The second reading isn't getting much support. The Conservatives have a free vote, meaning each MP can vote as they see fit. Labour uses the whip to vote the bill down, which some 70 MPs ignore and vote for it anyway.

Here's part of Heath's speech to the House of Commons:

'I believe that our friends (the EEC) would find it incomprehensible if we were to tear up the agreement - the very agreement we have struggled for more than a decade to achieve. For years to come they would understandably ask whether any trust could be placed in Britain's role in any future international agreements. Our influence in world monetary and trade discussions would be destroyed. These questions would be settled by the United States, the European Community and Japan. The Community would not be broken up if we were to defect. It would suffer a bitter shock, but it would survive and go on. But Britain would not benefit from the progress it was making.'

'I have dealt with many of the major issues raised in the debate. I will deal now in particular with one matter. As the House knows, I have always believed that our prosperity and our influence in the world would benefit from membership. I believed until recently that we could carry on fairly well outside, but I believe now that with developments in world affairs, and the speed at which they are moving, it will become more and more difficult for Britain alone.'

'Faced with this prospect of change, I do not believe that any prime minister could come to this House and say, "We have secured the chance to join the European Community; we have signed the Treaty of Accession; we have the opportunity of full membership; but I now advise this House to throw them away. I do not believe that any prime minister could say that, and it follows from what I have said that this Bill is not a luxury which we can dispense with if need be.'

'It has been a central policy of three successive governments, irrespective of party, and of all three main parties in this House that Britain should join the European Community if suitable arrangements could be negotiated. By a large majority this House decided in principle last October that Britain should join the Community on the basis of the arrangements negotiated by my Right Honourable and learned friend the Chancellor of the Duchy. Any Government which thereafter failed to give legislative effect to that clear decision of this House would be abdicating its responsibilities.'

'I must tell the House that my colleagues and I are of one mind that the Government cannot abdicate their responsibilities in this matter. Therefore, if this House will not agree to the Second Reading of the bill tonight and so refuses to give legislative effect to its own decision of principle, taken by a vast majority less than four months ago, my colleagues and I are unanimous that in these circumstances this Parliament cannot sensibly continue. I urge Honourable Members to implement the clear decision of principle taken on 28th October last and to cast their votes for the second reading of this bill.'

MPs vote narrowly in favour of the Bill 309-301

In a June 1972 interview with Ted Heath, it's clear that the country is in a mess. After only two years in power the problems are mounting. Prices are rising due to high inflation. High pay settlements as a result of strikes and mass unemployment are prevalent.

When it comes to joining the EEC, a poll suggests that the British public are either indifferent or hostile. Heath is of the opinion the polls are wrong and he believes the public are in favour of joining.

---

13 July 1972 - The third and final reading of the bill; MPs vote 301-284 in favour; it then passes to the House of Lords and receives Royal Assent on 17 October 1972.

When asked by a reporter about the vote in Parliament on the European Communities Act 1972, Heath gives the impression that an overwhelming number of MPs voted in favour of it.

> ## MPs vote in favour of the Bill by
> ## a narrow margin of 301-284

> ## THE BOTTOM LINE
>
> The Bill to ratify joining the EEC is passed by just 17 votes on the third reading.
>
> **Was there a case to hold a referendum?**

Edward Heath knows of EEC intentions

Edward Heath confirms in a speech that he is aware of EEC intentions to become a United States of Europe:

'The community which we are joining is far more than a common market. It is a community in the true sense of that term. It is concerned not only with the establishment of free trade, economic and monetary union and other major economic issues ...'. Ted Heath is personally involved in the negotiations because he believes membership will promote peace and stability between Britain and Europe.

> ## 1 January 1973 - Britain joins the Common Market

1973-1975 world recession hits hard

The booming 1960s come to an abrupt end as a world recession hits, exasperated by the 1973 oil crisis. The Organization of Arab Petroleum Exporting Countries (OPEC) places an embargo on those nations they think are supporting Israel during the Yom Kippur War (6-26 October 1973). The embargo initially targets Britain, the United States, Canada, Japan, and the Netherlands. By the end of the embargo in March 1974, the price of oil has risen nearly 400%, from $3 per barrel to nearly $12. Inflation peaks at 20%. A three-day working week is introduced in January 1974 as electricity is rationed due to fears of a power shortage as a result of a bitter miners' strike. They demand a 35% pay rise and reject an offer of a 16%. Edward Heath calls a snap election on 28 February 1974 and loses.

France is hit very hard by a severe currency shortage. They take the unusual step of limiting imports by only allowing goods in through one port. This causes chaos. Complaints are made that their actions contravenes EEC rules with regard to the free movement of goods.

February 1974 - Labour's minority government

Opinion polls give the Tories a comfortable win and get it wrong - again. Labour wins four seats more than the Conservatives. This results in a hung parliament.

Labour, who are 17 seats short of a majority refuses to form a coalition with Ted Heath, who then resigns as Party Leader.

Heath's resignation sees the MP for Finchley, Margaret Thatcher, become leader of the Opposition.

The new Prime Minister Harold Wilson gives coal miners a 29% wage rise to gain time to put his energy policy in place, which will result in mine closures decimating the industry.

As leader of the Labour Party Harold Wilson gives an interview on his winning manifesto and issues of the day. Right at the beginning he says: 'On food prices, apart from renegotiating the terms of entry into the Common Market, we will have strict price control ... We shall have food subsidies on the most important items in the housewife's family budget.' These are measures required to counteract the food price hike that resulted from implementing the CAP after joining the EEC a year earlier.

October 1974 - Labour win a clear majority

As expected, PM Wilson calls another snap election after finding it impossible to form a stable government. Labour wins 319 seats and beats Margaret Thatcher's Conservative Party, but has a majority of just one seat in the House.

Labour fought the election on a commitment to renegotiate the terms of EEC membership and to hold a referendum on whether to remain on renegotiated terms or to leave.

This is ironically the exact same tactic used by PM David Cameron and the basis for the 2016 referendum.

MP Enoch Powell (b. 1912, d. 1998), an outspoken Eurosceptic, leaves the Conservatives after denouncing Margaret Thatcher's policies on the Common Market. He wins the seat for South Down as one of only 12 members of the Ulster Unionist Party (which governed Northern Ireland 1921–1972).

May 1975 - Television plays an important role

There is a heated television debate on the forthcoming referendum between the former Conservative Prime Minister Edward Heath (pro-Europe) and Labour MP Michael Foot (Eurosceptic).

June 1975 - The first in-out referendum

The country is now under a Labour government led again by Harold Wilson. The Labour party is bitterly divided on Europe. The Labour manifesto calls for an in-out referendum to allow people the opportunity to decide whether Britain should stay in the Common Market on renegotiated terms or whether it should leave. The referendum takes place on 5 June 1975.

The renegotiation of terms revolves around payments to the CAP. Harold Wilson achieves some reductions to British payments, but the amount is minimal and the issue is still there. New Zealand is allowed market access for their dairy products. The European Regional Development Fund (ERDF) is created to help farmers in Britain's poorer regions. It is agreed that a 'corrective mechanism' that would apply to all countries in economic difficulties will be set up in May 1976. Britain will never benefit from the ERDF due to the discovery of North Sea oil which means Britain will contribute 20% of Community revenue but only receive 12% of its expenditure.

In hindsight, not what you would call a fantastic deal.

Harold Wilson runs a campaign to support remaining in the Community. He promotes the negotiated terms as a huge success. The new Leader of the Opposition, Margaret Thatcher, supports him wholeheartedly.

An interview in May 1975 with Labour Prime Minister Harold Wilson, who is riding a political high at the time, discusses the implications of the forthcoming referendum on 5 June 1975.

As a leader promoting a vote to remain, it is interesting how important the Commonwealth is to Wilson - who has just returned from a two-week Commonwealth conference. He says, 'Remember, I have never been an emotional European... I am an emotional Commonwealth man.' He goes on to say that it would certainly be a traumatic experience should Britain leave the EEC because a lot has happened in the last three years. He claims that Britain has been able to make changes to the agreement with the EEC.

Later on in the interview Wilson explains how the referendum has polarized the nation and Parliament.

Q: 'Mr Eric Deacon, Undersecretary at the Department of Trade, said that most major foodstuffs are costing Britain more than if we were outside the EEC. Is that true?'

Wilson gets flustered and attempts to deflect, then says: 'The food issue is a very important one and a difficult one, it is a fact that certainly we have not had to pay more for food as a result of being in the Market. Others might say that it's been a period of temporary higher prices. I am satisfied that we certainly couldn't have got our food cheaper anywhere else.'

He also mentions the butter and beef mountains caused by an over-production that is a direct result of the CAP.

MP Tony Benn (Lab) leads the 'Leave/No' camp. The smear campaign against Benn, by a press who supports 'remain', is vicious. He was tipped to become prime minister one day, which Wilson puts a stop to in subsequent years.

The title of one pamphlet for the 'Leave/No' campaign says: THE RIGHT TO RULE OURSELVES. The fundamental question is whether or not we remain free to rule ourselves in our own way. In a letter to his constituents 1975 which was published by The Spectator, Tony Benn wrote:

'Britain's continuing membership of the Community would mean the end of Britain as a completely self-governing nation and the end of our democratically elected parliament as the supreme law-making body in the United Kingdom.'

'I am, of course, not here addressing myself to the general political or economic arguments for or against entry, nor commenting on the view that the advantages of membership might outweigh the loss of democratic rights that I have described. But no one who votes in the ballot box should be in any doubt as to the effect British membership has had, and will increasingly continue to have, in removing the power the British people once enjoyed to govern themselves.'

'We must respect the sincerity of those who take a different view from our own. We should all accept the verdict of the British people whatever it is, and I shall certainly do so.'

Referendum result: 67.23% Remain - 32.77% Leave

March 1976 - Wilson resigns as Prime Minister

The recession had been officially declared over in 1975 but unemployment is the highest ever, topping the one million mark, strikes cripple the manufacturing and public service sectors, and inflation remains very high. PM Wilson resigns.

His successor, James Callaghan, takes a multibillion-pound bail-out from the International Monetary Fund (IMF) to bolster Britain's wavering economy. He attempts to renegotiate British contributions to Brussels yet again, but to no avail.

December 1976 - MP Enoch Powell makes his famous 'Rivers of Blood' speech to Parliament with some accurate predictions about the EEC.

March 1979 - Exchange rate mechanism created

The exchange rate mechanism (ERM) is launched to stabilize exchange rates across the EEC. This is the precursor to introducing a single currency. Participants of the ERM are obliged to keep their exchange rates within 2.25% on either side of a given exchange rate. It is pegged to the Deutschmark, which makes sense since Germany has the largest and most stable economy in Europe.

The Labour Chancellor of the Exchequer, MP Denis Healey (1974–1979, famous for his bushy eyebrows), is deeply concerned that, by tying EEC currencies to the Deutschmark, the ERM will benefit the German economy at the expense of other member countries. He was right!

All EEC states take part from day one - except Britain

The issue of Britain joining the ERM is discussed in Parliament no fewer than eight times between 1979 and 1990. After which a reluctant prime minister agrees to join, under pressure.

Britain joins the ERM October 1990 but is forced to exit just two years later as Germany increases interest rates and requests that Britain devalue the pound.

Denis Healey had predicted this danger ten years earlier. Britain pays a heavy price and never re-joins the exchange rate mechanism.

CHAPTER THREE

The Thatcher Years

The very mention of her name stirs passion in anyone who lived through the Thatcher years. People either admire her or hate her. As one of the most influential politicians in the European building process, her actions and ideas changed the face of EEC-British relations like no other leader.

Margaret Thatcher is a champion of the Eurosceptics, a defender of national sovereignty, and of the independence of EEC member states from European institutions.

Always conscious of the benefits to be derived from membership of the Common Market she has no intention of destroying the European building process. She simply wants to redirect it from supranational aspirations toward national cooperation.

Margaret Hilda Roberts was born in October 1925, in Grantham, a small town in Lincolnshire, England. Her father, Alfred Roberts, owns two grocery stores, is an active member of the local council, and is a Methodist preacher. He was also Mayor of Grantham for two years just after World War II.

Margaret Roberts wins a scholarship to study chemistry at Oxford University (1943-1947). Even then she shows an interest in politics becoming President of the Oxford University Conservative Association in 1946.

Two years later she joins the local Conservative Association and attends her first party conference in Llandudno, Wales. At the tender age of just 24 she is asked to become the Conservative candidate for Dartford (a safe Labour seat) in February 1949. At the celebratory dinner for winning the candidacy she meets Denis Thatcher. They get married three years later.

As the candidate for Dartford it makes sense to move there. She supports herself as a research chemist. She loses two elections (1950 and 1951) but nevertheless reduces the Labour majority by 7,000.

It takes ten years of hard work for her to claim a seat in Parliament, as MP for Finchley in October 1959.

Thirty years after standing for Dartford, she becomes the longest-serving British Prime Minister of the 20th century.

May 1979 - Conservatives win the election

Thatcher tables and wins a vote of no confidence, forcing Labour PM Jim Callaghan to call an election. The country is still reeling from the 'winter of discontent' with high inflation (17%), drawn-out strikes, and unemployment at 1.56 million. All this damages Labour's standing in the polls. The Conservatives gain 62 seats, Labour loses 50. The SNP, with 71 candidates, only wins two seats. Who remembers the slogan 'Labour isn't Working'?

The Conservatives take back power with Margaret Thatcher, the first female prime minister, at the helm.

She arrives at 10 Downing Street for the first time and gives a short interview that mentions the assassination (car bomb) of her campaign manager MP Mr Airey Neave.

She also quotes from St. Francis of Assisi: 'Where there is discord, may we bring harmony. Where there is error, may we bring truth. Where there is doubt, may we bring faith. And where there is despair, may we bring hope.'

The incoming government inherits a country in trouble and bankrupt. The problems it needs to resolve include tackling inflation, reducing the national debt, which is 44.5% of GDP, and getting the ever striking trade unions in line.

Although Britain is the third-poorest country in the EEC (Germany and France are richer) it is nevertheless required to make a net contribution to EEC coffers of £1 billion per year (equivalent to £10 billion in 2020), which is far more than other countries but in return for less.

Thatcher goes about the task of sorting out Britain's finances by raising interest rates to 17% and cutting public spending. This isn't popular as it causes unemployment to double to three million within five years. A deep recession ensues.

Thatcher decides to sell off council houses to raise money - many council estates are run down and the cost of maintenance outweighs the income from rents. The Right to Buy policy comes into force in 1980. In 1981, 66,321 purchases are made and 174,697 in 1982. The sales bring in £692 million in 1980/1, £1.4 billion in 1981/2 and £1.98 billion in 1982/3. This helps put fiscal Britain back on track.

An oversupply of milk products in the marketplace hits the news again - dubbed 'the butter mountain'.

Declassified documents published by the National Archives give an insight as to how Mrs Thatcher feels about the Common Fisheries Policy. In September 1979 she notes:

'The fisheries situation was already sufficiently unsatisfactory without our making further concessions. The so-called reciprocity of historic sights was meaningless since the French had fished out their own waters and British access to those waters was worthless.'

June 1983 - Thatcher elected for a second term

Conservatives have 397 seats, Labour has 209. This is the largest parliamentary majority of the post-war era. Thatcher is on a roll and Thatcherism the new buzz word. She now has the mandate to radically change a nation.

It's a crippling defeat for the Labour Party led by Michael Foot whose manifesto calls for leaving the EEC without a referendum. In a campaign speech Tony Blair told voters; "We'll negotiate withdrawal from the EEC, which has drained our natural resources and destroyed jobs."

No fewer than three future Labour Party leaders take their seats in Parliament for the first time: Tony Blair (Lab), MP for Sedgefield; Gordon Brown (Lab), MP for Dunfermline East; and Jeremy Corbyn (Lab), MP for Islington North.

June 1984 - 66% British rebate agreed

At Fontainebleau outside Paris, Margaret Thatcher successfully negotiates a multibillion pound rebate of 66%, to be given back to Britain from EEC contributions. Her famous words going into the negotiations: 'We are not asking for a penny piece of Community money for Britain. What we are asking is for a very large amount of our own money back.'

Lord Owens comment, 'The arithmetic was really bad for Britain', sums up the true situation in the country, created by the implementation of the Common Agricultural Policy CAP.

1984-1985 Miners' strike

A once-proud, nationalized coal mining industry becomes unprofitable as a result of alternative energy, such as nuclear power, North Sea natural gas, and cheaper coal from abroad. Pit closures are inevitable.

Union leader Arthur Scargill leads 187,000 mineworkers, angry about mass pit closures that follow the government's withdrawal of subsidies. The National Union of Miners (NUM) fails to hold a ballot of its members, so the strike is ruled illegal in September 1984. However, it continues to 3 March 1985. The government eventually wins and by 2009 only six working pits remain in the UK, compared to 174 in 1983.

What makes this strike so memorable is the strength of emotions and the violence against those workers who refuse to strike. Strike breakers are called scabs and strike supporters, called flying pickets, are bussed to producing collieries. Over 12 months' six people die and 11,300 are arrested. The biggest clashes between pickets and police are at Orgreave Colliery.

October 1984 - IRA Brighton bombing

The IRA planted an explosive device at the Grand Hotel in Brighton during the Conservative Party conference targeting PM Margaret Thatcher and her Cabinet. Thatcher escaped unhurt but the blast killed five people including MP, Sir Anthony Berry (Deputy Chief Whip), Lady Shattock wife of Sir Gordon Shattock, MP Eric Taylor and wounding 30 others.

January 1985 - How people see the EEC

The bumpy road to British-EEC harmonization is highlighted by a fantastic debate between two MEPs, David Curry (Con) and Bob Cryer (Lab, Eurosceptic), and a very well informed pro-European, Kenneth Williams (of Carry On fame) in front of a highly emotional European and British audience.

The issues and opinions expressed in 1985 don't differ from the concerns and prejudices people have in 2016. MEP Bob Cryer's talk of reform, and some of the opinions expressed, demonstrate how long this discussion has been going on. It's always a pleasure to watch Kenneth Williams.

June 1985 - Schengen Treaty signed

This Treaty is an agreement to get rid of controls at common borders. It is signed near the small town of Schengen in Luxembourg. There is a lack of consensus among members and only five of the ten member states are signatories: France, West Germany, Belgium, Luxembourg, and the Netherlands. Britain doesn't sign up and opts out completely, as does Ireland.

Schengen becomes a core part of EU law in 1999, whereby all members are legally obliged to sign up for it. The UK and Ireland retain their option to opt out.

February 1985 - Greenland votes to leave the EEC

Greenland who was granted home rule in 1979 by Denmark holds an in-out referendum February 1982. 53% vote to leave the EEC. The result is hardly surprising as 70% voted against joining in 1972; back then as a county of Denmark where 63% were for join, this left Greenland with little say in the matter.

Grøxit, that's not something you say after someone sneezes, it's their version of Brexit. This is the first time a sovereign territory votes to leave the EEC. Their main gripe is with the Common Fisheries Policy and control over Greenland's fish resources, especially shrimps and prawns. Other countries are fishing in their waters and depleting stocks.

The ensuing Treaty refers to Greenland as a 'special case' with regard to its supranational European affiliation and the country is later granted OCT-status.

Overseas Countries and Territories Association OCT

This Association, founded in 2000, promotes the economic and social development of the OCTs and their close economic relations with the Community. The EU grants unilateral trade preferences (duty-free quota-free access to the EU) to all products originating in the OCTs. The rules of origin stipulate the conditions under which this preferential access is to be enjoyed by the beneficiary countries.

You could say, it's cherry picking.

February 1986 - Single European Act signed

To launch an ambitious plan to create a single market, the Single European Act (SEA) comes into force on 1 July 1987 as a precursor to the European Community (EC). This is the first major revision of the 1957 Treaty of Rome. It gives legislative powers to the European Parliament for the first time and heralds the free movement of goods, capital, labour, and services known as 'the four freedoms'.

It is ratified by the British Parliament, without consulting the British people. After signing this treaty Thatcher becomes sceptical of the overall EEC project because of policies that are leading toward a monetary union.

The Danish parliament rejects it believing the Act gives too much power to the European Parliament. But a Danish referendum, held in February 1986, approves the treaty.

The Italians delay signing it for the opposite reason, as it doesn't give enough powers to the European Parliament.

The Irish hold a referendum May 1987 because signing it requires a change in their constitution - 69.9% vote in favour, with a turnout of just 44.1%.

Spain, Portugal and Greece emerge from dictatorships in the 1970s. A 'democratic' Greece joined the EEC in January 1981, followed by Spain and Portugal in 1986. The northern Mediterranean is now part of the EEC.

June 1987 - Thatcher is elected for a third term

There's a notable rise in people's living standards due to the policies of the previous two terms. Inflation is only 4%, (lowest level in 20 years), there is a strong economy, and lower taxes. A landslide victory for the Conservative Party (376 seats to Labour's 229) is hardly surprising.

Margaret Thatcher becomes the first prime minister in 160 years to win three successive terms in office. She has earned the title of Iron Lady and continues with the ideology named after her, Thatcherism.

The former Labour Prime Minister James Callaghan and MP Enoch Powell lose their seats, never to return to politics.

Alex Salmond (SNP) arrives on the scene. He wins the seat for Banff and Buchan with 44.3% of the votes. Just three years later he becomes leader of the Scottish National Party and a First Minister of Scotland (2007-2014).

September 1988 - Thatcher's Bruges speech

On 21 September 1988 Margaret Thatcher delivers a speech about her vision for future relationships between Britain and Europe. This was her response to the first draft of what was to become the Maastricht Treaty. She is concerned about a power grab by the European Commission. The speech is her attempt to persuade EEC policy makers to change course.

It's a clear message to the attending senior EEC officials that she will oppose any attempt to turn the EEC into an economic and political union. She lays down five guiding principles. Here are some excerpts from her speech.

Thatcher's five guiding principles

1. Willing cooperation between sovereign states

'My first guiding principle is this: willing and active cooperation between independent sovereign states is the best way to build a successful European Community.'

The operative words here are willing and independent sovereign states - in other words, not becoming a United States of Europe. She went on to say:

'Europe will be stronger precisely because it has France as France, Spain as Spain, Britain as Britain, each with its own customs, traditions and identity. It would be folly to try to fit them into some sort of identikit European personality.'

2. Encouraging change

'My second guiding principle is this: Community policies must tackle present problems in a practical way, however difficult that may be.'

'If we cannot reform those Community policies which are patently wrong (referring to CAP) or ineffective and which are rightly causing public disquiet, then we shall not get the public support for the Community's future development.'

'It was not right that half the total Community budget was being spent on storing and disposing of surplus food (referring to the butter mountain caused by CAP) ... Now those stocks are being sharply reduced (price dumping due to a surplus, which ruins the livelihoods of British farmers).'

3. Europe open to enterprise

'My third guiding principle is the need for Community policies which encourage enterprise.'

'That a state-controlled economy is a recipe for low growth and that free enterprise within a framework of law brings better results.'

'Of course, we must make it easier for people to travel throughout the Community. But it is a matter of plain common sense that we cannot totally abolish frontier controls if we are also to protect our citizens from crime and stop the movement of drugs, of terrorists and of illegal immigrants.'

4. Europe open to the world

'My fourth guiding principle is that Europe should not be protectionist.'

5. Europe and defence

'My last guiding principle concerns the most fundamental issue - the European countries' role in defence. Europe must continue to maintain a sure defence through NATO.'

'But let us never forget that our way of life, our vision and all we hope to achieve, is secured not by the rightness of our cause but by the strength of our defence.'

'On this, we must never falter, never fail.'

Summing up the British approach

'Mr Chairman, I believe it is not enough just to talk in general terms about a European vision or ideal. If we believe in it, we must chart the way ahead and identify the next steps. And that is what I have tried to do this evening.'

1988 - EEC regional aid doubled

Market liberalization helped northern European members to become richer. Poorer southern states, such as Greece (joining 1981), Spain, and Portugal (joining 1986) demand compensation. This comes in the form of a cohesion policy through which thousands of projects receive huge financial support from structural funds. The money helps to construct roads, bridges, factories, airports - designed to aid regional development.

October 1990 - Britain becomes party to the ERM

Britain reluctantly joins the exchange rate mechanism 11 years after it is created to stabilize exchange rates within the EEC.

The growth and scale of export/import businesses is moving into the billions of pounds each year. This requires a stable rate of exchange so that businesses know how much they will receive or pay out for goods or services when dealing with other countries. With the pound floating freely against all other currencies, businesses could never be sure how much they would be paying for something in the future. A fluctuating exchange rate can cause the price to be significantly higher or lower.

During the 1980s there are heated discussions between the Chancellor of the Exchequer, Nigel Lawson, and Margaret Thatcher who is against the ERM. Lawson resigns in 1989. He is replaced by John Major, who now persuades Thatcher to join. Politicians are enthusiastic, believing it will lower inflation and move Britain closer to European integration, giving it more influence. The effect of Britain joining the ERM is immediate: interest rates drop for the first time in a year; there is a massive rise in share prices; the value of the pound increases.

Altering the interest rate is the tool available to governments to ensure that their currency will stay within ERM bandwidths.

November 1990 - Thatcher ousted as prime minister

Two years after giving her famous Bruges speech, she is in Parliament condemning Europe's approach to building the union in her 'no, no, no' speech on 30 October 1990.

She isn't hiding her hostility toward the Common Market which upsets her pro-Europe government. This anti-EEC rhetoric eventually leads to her downfall opening the way for Conservatives to sign the Maastricht Treaty that she won't.

Douglas Hurd, who is sitting directly to her left during her speech, is one of the signatories of the Maastricht Treaty.

Conservative MPs, feeling bullied by Thatcher for so many years, are not happy and about to revolt. The Deputy Chief Whip, Lord Garel-Jones, had warned Thatcher a year earlier to soften her anti-European rhetoric and had asked her to reconsider her highly unpopular flagship policy (community charge or poll tax) to help improve MPs' re-election chances. He said, 'There are a hundred assassins lurking in the bushes and in a year's time they are going to come out and kill you!' How right he is.

Her popularity takes a massive hit as the economy sees a downturn, inflation rises, and interest rates increase.

A chain of events triggered by the resignation of Deputy Prime Minister Geoffrey Howe just two days after Thatcher's 'no, no, no' speech - goes down in history as the biggest betrayal of any leader in British history.

1 November 1990 - Geoffrey Howe resigns

In a Cabinet reshuffle July 1989, Geoffrey Howe (Con) is sacked as Foreign Secretary and replaced by John Major. This also means giving up the Foreign Secretary's country residence, Chevening, a luxury 15-bedroom mansion in Kent.

Howe is then appointed Leader of the House of Commons, Lord President of the Council and Deputy Prime Minister. You might think this is a promotion but, it isn't.

Geoffrey Howe resigns on 1 November 1990, just two days after Thatcher's 'no, no, no' speech.

Howe believes deeply in European unity, and gives a scathing resignation speech criticizing Thatcher's resolve to halting further EEC integration. He points out how different the relationship might have been if Britain had signed the Treaty of Rome in 1957, which would have given Britain more control from the onset.

His resignation speech triggers a series of events that happen at breakneck speed causing a bid for the leadership, which Thatcher believes she can easily win.

Geoffrey Howe gives up being an MP at the April 1992 general election and is made a life peer in June that year, which gives him a seat in the House of Lords. He retires in May 2015 and dies just five months later.

Heseltine's bid for the leadership

Thatcher hears that Michael Heseltine is drumming up support for a leadership contest. She confronts him with an ultimatum, 'put up or shut up' - a war cry that John Major uses some years later when faced with a similar challenge.

Confident she will win a leadership challenge, she brings forward the election contest date to 20 November 1990. She wants to get it over with quickly to limit any damage it may do to the Party.

Heseltine, spurred on by Howe's resignation speech, picks up the gauntlet on 14 November announcing his intention to stand against Thatcher in a leadership contest.

20 Nov. 1990 - Round one, let the contest begin

The Conservative Party leadership election is to take place on 20 November 1990. There are only six days to prepare... The race is on.

Thatcher agrees not to campaign personally; she avoids television and radio. She only gives two press interviews, in both of which, when the issue of a single currency is raised, she says firmly that she is prepared to put the issue to the people.

As her Party goes about deciding her fate she keeps to her busy schedule as prime minister: visits troops in Northern Ireland on 16 November; attends the European Summit in

Paris from 19-21 November, hobnobs with world leaders and signs the Paris Charter. She wants to give an impression of confidence and is still in Paris on the day voting takes place.

Michael Heseltine is a serious contender. A millionaire by 35 and a Cabinet member at 41, he'd never thought Margaret Thatcher as leadership material and couldn't understand how she'd got the votes in the 1974 election. He is contemptuous of her working-class background.

His last Cabinet post was as Defence Secretary (1983-1986). A scandal involving Westland helicopters - leaked letters and a desire to keep them British or bust - forced him to resign. In his resignation speech he referred to Thatcher as a liar who lacked integrity. He has been a backbencher now for four years and hankers for the crown, and this is his one and only chance to get it.

Thatcher gets more votes than Heseltine, receiving 204 to his 152 votes from Tory MPs, she doesn't win. Parliamentary rules require that the winner gets 15% more votes than their opponent. The margin of her victory is just four votes short of the 15% rule. A second election must take place.

She consults with her Cabinet, then withdraws from the race. You would think that this surely makes Heseltine the natural winner. MP Cecil Parkinson says, 'She stepped aside to let John Major or Douglas Hurd win.'

27 Nov. 1990 - Round two - the more the merrier

Cabinet members don't want Heseltine (a backbencher) as PM and decide that only a Cabinet member should succeed. They allow two new contenders to enter the race, blocking Heseltine from being pronounced winner forcing a second election on 27 November 1990. The line-up is:

Michael Heseltine	Pro-Europe
Douglas Hurd	Pro-Europe (signs Maastricht Treaty)
John Major	Pro-Europe (signs Maastricht Treaty)

Thatcher lobbies hard in support of John Major, who receives most votes (49.7%), still two votes short of the 15% rule. As the result is announced Heseltine and Hurd withdraw their candidacies. The most unlikely candidate with the least experience wins. Enter the new prime minister, John Major.

In Thatcher's final speech to the House of Commons on 22 November 1990, she is still fighting the cause as she says to Labour Opposition Leader Neil Kinnock, 'On the central issues of Europe's future they will not tell us where they stand. Do they want a single currency? The Right Honourable Gentleman doesn't even know what it means ...' She continues, 'The fact is that Britain has done more to shape the Community over the past 11 years than any other member state. Britain is leading the reform of the Common Agricultural Policy, getting surpluses down, putting a ceiling on agricultural spending...'

A final twist to a sorry tale

On the morning of 22 November 1990, Margaret Thatcher announces her decision to stand down as prime minister. That afternoon, Labour tables a vote of no confidence which, curiously, she wins with an overwhelming vote of confidence. Losing this vote might have triggered a general election.

BRIEF TIMELINE

30 Oct. 1990 - Thatcher gives her 'no, no, no' speech

1 Nov. 1990 - Geoffrey Howe resigns

14 Nov. 1990 - Michael Heseltine's leadership bid

20 Nov. 1990 - First round of leadership elections

22 Nov. 1990 - Thatcher concedes defeat and resigns

27 Nov. 1990 - Second round of leadership elections -
as his two opponents withdraw,
John Major is elected PM.

After being deposed, Margaret Thatcher continues as a backbencher MP and is not silenced on the issue of the EU.

The question in my mind is whether she would have created a different dynamic in today's Britain if she'd not been ousted by a handful of her party. In my opinion, her negotiating skills would have given Britain a better position within Europe.

Thatcher gives up her seat in the Commons just before the 1992 general elections. She becomes a member of the House of Lords in the same year and makes a series of speeches criticizing the Maastricht Treaty, describing it as 'a treaty too far' and states:

'I could never have signed this treaty.'

In 2003 Thatcher publishes a book called ,Statecraft', in which she said that Britain should leave the Common Market.

Feb. 1991 - Assassination attempt on John Major

The Provisional Irish Republican Army (IRA) launch three homemade mortar shells at the HQ of the Government of the United Kingdom. It was an assassination attempt on Prime Minister John Major and his Cabinet. Fortunately, the assassination attempt failed and nobody was killed.

November 1991 - UKIP is created

Alan Sked MP, a Eurosceptic who believes that the EEC is corrupt, anti-democratic, and a risk to the British economy, forms the Anti-Federalist League (AFL) in London. It is renamed the UK Independence Party (UKIP) two years later in September 1993.

BOOK TWO

THE
POST-THATCHER
YEARS

(1992 - 2016)

INTRODUCTION

Lest We Forget

Margaret Thatcher fought hard for Britain's position within Europe, trying to outwit countries that had set up an institution designed to work in their own interests, which was not necessarily good for Britain.

Like in a Shakespearean tragedy, she is dethroned in an unceremonious manner by those closest to her. The conspirators persuade Thatcher's Foreign Secretary, Geoffrey Howe, to lead the plot to stop her from scuppering the EU master plan. Lord Heseltine seizes his chance to be king but fails to take the throne, losing the joust to the grey knave, John Major.

Well, maybe not quite so dramatic - but Britain is now in a post-Thatcher era.

The tabling of the most comprehensive and far-reaching treaty the EEC had ever constructed is about to be thrust upon a very willing new leader. The annexation of Britain by the EU is in full swing and given the green light by Parliament. Yet again, the Government of the day, led by John Major, doesn't see the need to consult the British people about a treaty of such magnitude.

John Major was born and raised in the South of England, his first job was working for an insurance broker. He couldn't find decent work so took a correspondence course in banking, which got him a job in a bank in 1965. In 1959, aged 16, he joined the Young Conservatives in Brixton. In 1964 he stood as a candidate for Lambeth Borough Council, and was elected as a councillor in 1968. Up until 1971 he was Chairman of the Housing Committee, overseeing several housing estate developments in Lambeth.

Major's first attempt to stand for parliament is for St. Pancras North in the February and October 1974 elections – he is defeated on both occasions. In May 1979 he is selected for the safe Conservative seat of Huntingdon and enters parliament for the first time - just as Thatcher becomes prime minister.

After just two years as an MP, he's appointed as parliamentary private secretary, then to assistant whip in 1983, Under Secretary of State for Social Security in 1985, then Minister of State for the same department a year later. A whirlwind career.

John Major is offered his first Cabinet position after retaining his seat in the 1987 elections. Just ten years after becoming an MP, Thatcher offers him Geoffrey Howe's job as Foreign Secretary then appoints him as Chancellor of the Exchequer just three months later, in October 1989 (that correspondence course in banking must have sealed the deal). In the space of just two years he's gone from junior minister to securing two top Cabinet positions.

CHAPTER FOUR

THE MAJOR
ERRORS

December 1991 - Signing the draft Maastricht Treaty

A country in recession with rising unemployment now has a less than charismatic prime minister at the helm (compared to his predecessor). John Major has a lot on his plate.

Major's claim to power on 27 November 1990 is the pinnacle of a whirlwind career spanning just three years. He is not leader through a democratic process and the support of the British electorate, but through a Conservative Party vote to replace the Eurosceptic Margaret Thatcher - who would never have signed the Maastricht Treaty. She's a tough act to follow. Major, a pro-Europe supporter, is about to sign a treaty that will take Britain to the next level.

John Major sees no reason to call a referendum to ratify the Maastricht Treaty, despite calls from his party, and a bill passing through parliament by just 17 votes in favour. On 11 December 1991, 12 months after taking office, John Major signs the draft Maastricht Treaty (MT) that turns the EEC into the EU. 'Game, set and match for Britain,' is what he is supposed to have said.

The irony is, that some 28 years later in 2019 the very same John Major is fighting the case for a second referendum - when he hadn't even offered an unsuspecting public one referendum before signing a treaty giving up sovereignty.

THE CRUX OF IT

No referendum to join but let's have two referendums if the people decide they want to leave, just to be sure.

The EEC (Market) is converted into the EU (Union)

The Maastricht Treaty, among other things, paves the way for monetary union and includes a chapter on social policy (workers' rights). Major negotiates an opt-out on both issues. In parliament, Labour and the Liberal Democrats oppose the opt-out to the social policy but to no avail. The treaty also introduces 'European citizenship' giving Europeans the right to live and work, and to vote in elections, in any EU country.

A brief guide to the Maastricht Treaty

The President of France, Francois Mitterrand (1981-1995) and the German chancellor, Dr. Helmut Kohl (1982-1988) who received the title 'Honorary citizen of Europe' in December 1998, are both instrumental in the creation of the Maastricht Treaty. Kohl's life's work revolves around the unification of Germany, the improvement of cooperation between European countries, and the creation of an economic and monetary union. In short, his vision is a politically integrated Europe. Realizing this gives Germany the means of achieving a second German industrial miracle - it had enjoyed the first just after World War II.

As with every previous EEC treaty the Maastricht Treaty is constructed mainly by Germany and France. It replaces or amends all previous treaties and changes the 'community' into a 'union' based on three pillars, or policies.

1. The Single European Act

This is really an extension of the Single European Act (SEA) agreed in February 1986. No duties on imports/exports and no EU borders. One of the biggest changes sees the European Parliament gaining more powers over member states.

2. A common foreign and security policy

This is probably one of the most difficult parts for member states to deal with. For example, after Yugoslavia split in 1990, member states couldn't agree on whether to recognize the newly created states; neither could they decide where to relocate migrants entering via Italy or Greece.

3. Cooperation on justice and home affairs

This covers things like, judicial cooperation in criminal and civil matters; the creation of a European Police Office (Europol); and combating terrorism, serious crime, drug trafficking, and international fraud.

In real terms this signals an intention to:

1. establish a European Union with no internal borders

2. lay the foundations for a single currency (euro)

3. create a common citizenship - the EU Passport

4. give greater euro-parliamentary powers to Brussels

5. create a common foreign and defence policy

6. promote closer cooperation to fight crime

7. introduce a central banking system

April 1992 - Conservatives win the election

The Conservatives led by John Major retain control of the Government for a fourth consecutive term against all the odds. They win by 336 seats to Labour's 271 – the opinion polls had favoured the Labour Leader Neil Kinnock.

The country goes deeper into recession - Major is not going to have an easy tenure. Five months into his term a decision that he had advised Thatcher to take on board comes back to bite him in the ass and explodes in his face.

Sept. 1992 - Black Wednesday, a sorry ERM tale

Under pressure from John Major, Britain joined the Exchange Rate Mechanism (ERM) when the country was on the verge of a recession and the pound was overvalued by around 10%.

Uncertainty over the Danish and French referendums is just one of the causes of the turmoil affecting the currency markets. International currency speculators begin to sell off sterling, devaluing it below the mandatory limits set out by the ERM. Attempts to prop it up cost the Government an estimated £3 billion from Britain's reserves, forcing a rise in interest rates to 15%. The pound is suspended from the ERM on 16 September 1992, never to return.

Maastricht Treaty Ratification by all Members

Remember that peculiarity of a treaty being signed first then ratification by Parliament being sought? The Maastricht Treaty is no different. After John Major signed the draft Maastricht Treaty December 1991 he now goes to Parliament for ratification.

From the 12 countries who sign the draft treaty in December 1991, only four hold a referendum, as was required by their respective constitutions:

➢ Italy (advisory) on May 1989 - 88.1% in favour

➢ Ireland on 18 June 1992 - 69.1% in favour

➢ France on 20 September 1992 - 50.8% in favour

➢ Denmark on 2 June 1992 - rejected by 50.7%.

Denmark rejects The Maastricht Treaty

The treaty can only come into effect if all 12 member states ratify it. The rejection from Denmark poses a real threat to the project and has to be resolved quickly. Denmark successfully negotiates opt-outs on the single currency, defence integration, citizenship rights and home affairs. These amendments are called the Edinburgh Agreement.

Denmark holds a second referendum on 18 May 1993 on the basis of the four opt-outs outlined above - 56.7% now vote in favour of the treaty.

The British Parliament is not obliged to seek approval by referendum as they have the doctrine of parliamentary sovereignty with legislative powers. This means they hold a debate, then vote for or against the issue themselves.

Parliament decides on treaty implementation

The draft treaty outlining the agreement was passed by Parliament December 1991 with a majority of only 17 votes.

It's now up to the PM John Major to get full parliamentary approval to the Maastricht Treaty through a series of votes and amendments in the House of Commons. It was never going to be easy as the Conservatives only have an 18-seat majority, meaning that every single vote will count.

Enter the Maastricht Rebels

The Conservative Eurosceptic faction is growing in numbers and lobbying hard against the treaty. They even risk having the whip withdrawn by voting with the Opposition and against their own Government to defeat bills. They also draw up some 400 amendments to the treaty and have some success getting them implemented. Labour also tables lots of amendments in an attempt to align it to their social and economic policies.

The Maastricht Rebels insist that if a referendum is held, they will stop trying to block the treaty. A referendum is repeatedly ruled out by John Major and his Government.

On the really big issues that the rebels oppose - like opting out of the 'Social Chapter' that covers workers' pay, health, and safety - they're unable to wield any influence.

There are some 20-plus core Maastricht Rebels - one of whom is Margaret Thatcher, who has stayed on as a backbencher MP after her ousting. With a House majority of only 18 seats this gives the rebels immense power when it comes to any vote. Here are some of the rebels who go on to prominent positions within Government in later years: Alan Duncan, Liam Fox, John Biffen, Bill Walker, Michael Spicer, Peter Tapsell, Iain Duncan Smith, Andrew Hunter, George Gardiner, Barry Legg. Bill Cash, Roger Knapman, Christopher Gill, Teresa Gorman and Richard Body go on to join UKIP.

In May 2016 Sir Iain Duncan Smith is asked about his reasons for voting against the Maastricht Treaty:

'The reason I voted against Maastricht all those years ago was because I felt, if we passed Maastricht, all its QMD (qualified majority voting) which enabled us to be outvoted in key areas, what we would see then was a process that would just continue to make that worse, I said at the time, that if we did that, then there would be only one decision to make, finally which is, do we stay in the EU or do we agree to lose our sovereign position as a nation-state, because so much of our lawmaking power, our democracy, would be taken away...'

One of the rebels' first successes is seen in March 1993 voting against their own party passing an amendment by 22 votes to ensure that anybody sitting on any European Community committee must be a duly elected representative. This amendment failed to avoid a situation highlighted by

Nigel Farage (MEP) on 24 February 2010, questioning the legality of the method by which the first permanent President of the EU Council, Herman Van Rompuy (2009-2014) had come into office. Rompuy, had not been duly elected to the position and was previously completely unknown politically.

Nigel Farage: 'We were told that when we had a president, we'd see a giant global political figure, a man who would be the political leader for 500 million people, the man that would represent all of us on the world stage, the man whose job was so important that of course you're paid more than President [Barack] Obama.'

Nigel Farage continues: 'Well, I'm afraid what we got was you (Rompuy) .. I don't want to be rude but, really, you have the charisma of a damp rag and the appearance of a low-grade bank clerk and the question I want to ask is, Who are you? I'd never heard of you. Nobody in Europe had ever heard of you.'

'I can speak on behalf of the majority of British people in saying that we don't know you, we don't want you, and the sooner you are put out to grass, the better.'

Farage adds, 'I have no doubt that your intention is to be the quiet assassin of European democracy and of European nation states.'

July 1993 - Maastricht Treaty end game

Ratification of the Maastricht Treaty (MT) comes to a head. There is a final stumbling block, which is resolved with a brilliant trick: make acceptance of the bill a question of confidence in the Government. If the bill now fails it will trigger an election, which risks the Conservatives losing power as they're popularity wanes.

On 6 May, Liberal Democrats win a Conservative safe seat in the Newbury by-election with a massive swing of 28.4%.

The Labour opposition tables an amendment on 22 July 1993 to postpone incorporation of the Treaty until the Government adopts the Social Chapter. The result is a tie - Ayes 317, Noes 317. The Speaker of the House, Betty Boothroyd (Lab) casts the deciding vote. The amendment to delay the treaty fails allowing it to progress. The Government then loses their main motion in the Maastricht ratification debate as MPs block it by 324 to 316. The next day, 23 July 1993, John Major tables an emergency confidence motion, worded as follows:

'This House has confidence in the policy of the Government on the adoption of the protocol on social policy.'

Instead of a vote for the bill it becomes a vote of confidence in the Government. MPs feel held to ransom over a bill they're not in favour of. Government wins by 40 votes. All the rebels vote for the bill, only MP Rupert Allason (Con) abstains, the whip is withdrawn as punishment.

Why the Social Chapter was a deal breaker

The opt-out of the Social Chapter negotiated by John Major is one of the main issues of concern to the Maastricht Rebels. The Labour and Liberal Democrat leaders also feel strongly that anything to do with the protection of workers' rights should be included in the treaty.

The Tory Government feels it would cost companies too much to implement and since they'd already successfully negotiated the opt-out with Brussels they just needed ratification by Parliament.

In May 1997 Labour's Foreign Secretary, Robin Cook, finally signs up to just two directives within the Social Chapter:

1. The Works Council directive, which requires employers to consult employees before making major changes in the workplace.

2. The Parental Leave directive, which specifies that parents should be allowed a maximum of three months unpaid leave after the birth of a child, to be taken over eight years.

July 1993 - Legal action to stop ratification of MT

Lord Rees-Mogg (father of Jacob Rees-Mogg MP, Con) launches a legal action a week after the bill is passed by the Commons in an attempt to stop Major's Government ratifying the Maastricht Treaty. The High Court rules in favour of the

Government on all three counts, which removes the last obstacle to ratification.

The Conservatives are beginning to lose seats at by-elections. On 29 July 1993 the constituency of Christchurch, a Conservative safe seat with a majority of 23,000, is lost to the Liberal Democrats with them gaining a majority of 16,000.

November 1993 - The Maastricht Treaty in force

From its signing in February 1992, it only took 21 months for 12 countries to ratify the Treaty. The EEC is now called the EU.

With the acceptance of the Maastricht Treaty on 1 November 1993 the EU can push ahead with its plans to implement a single currency (but not in the UK or Denmark).

'A referendum is a contradiction in a parliamentary democracy. We are elected to do the job.'

Douglas Hurd MP

BRIEF TIMELINE

11 December 1991 - John Major signs a draft of the MT

7 February 1992 - Douglas Hurd signs MT on behalf of UK

April 1992 - Conservatives win elections for a fourth term

21 May 1992 - 2nd reading MT Government wins 336 – 92

2 June 1992 - Denmark rejects the MT in a referendum

1 July 1992 - Britain has presidency of the EEC for 6 months

16 September 1992 - Britain forced to pull out of the ERM

18 May 1993 - Denmark approves MT in a 2nd referendum

20 May 1993 - Government wins 3rd reading of MT 292-112

20 July 1993 - House of Lords approves the MT by 141 - 29

23 July 1993 - Government wins confidence vote on MT

2 August 1993 - Parliament ratifies MT with all other states

1 November 1993 - The Maastricht Treaty takes effect

The Concept of the Whip

The whip system has been around since 1884. Selected MPs or Members of the House of Lords can be a whip and their supervisor is the Chief Whip. Their task is to ensure that party members vote in alignment with party policies.

Whips have to inform MPs about up coming debates and instruct them on how the party expects them to vote. They do this by sending out a letter (called The Whip) each week to all MPs. The Whip, lists future debates and rates them by importance, indicated by the number of underlines used.

This method of bloc voting helps promote discipline among MPs. You might consider this to be undemocratic but it's an attempt to get MPs to vote for policies Government was voted in on and not on the personal beliefs of each MP.

This system of underlining has three levels:

One-line whip - or one underline.
This is only an advisory guideline with no consequences for those MPs who don't attend or vote. Should they decide to vote they are expected to vote as instructed.

Two-line whip - or two underlines.
These are more serious and MP's attendance is 'necessary'. They are expected to vote as instructed and not doing so is frowned upon.

Three-line whip - or three underlines.

This is a mandatory instruction to vote. The debate is very important to the party and is mostly reserved for votes on second readings of major bills or for votes of confidence.

The consequences for MPs who defy a three-line whip can be severe. This is where the term 'having the whip withdrawn' comes in, essentially sacking an MP from the party, making them an independent until the whip is restored and they are let back into the party. Having the whip withdrawn can also mean losing your place in the Cabinet or being deselected, which means being sacked from the party altogether. Cabinet members are expected to resign first if they wish to vote against a three-line whip.

There have been occasions when whole groups of MPs have defied a three-line whip, resulting in them all having the whip withdrawn - as when John Major is faced with a vote of confidence or, later on, with Boris Johnson when 21 MPs abstain.

When the party in power has a small majority in the House then the whips' job becomes much more important and disciplinary actions can be more severe.

May 1994 - Channel Tunnel officially open

Agreed in principle in 1876, Her late Majesty Queen Elizabeth II and French President Mitterrand open the Channel Tunnel on 6 May 1994.

June 1994 - European Parliament elections

The Conservative Government is becoming more and more unpopular as crisis after crisis hits. John Major, with a 'wait and see' attitude, is undecided on whether to join the euro. His critics believe that ruling out the single currency altogether may cost them the next election.

Elections to the European Parliament (EP) on 9 June 1994 are a disaster for the Conservatives, who get the lowest share of votes in a national election since 1832.

Labour is the clear winner getting 62 seats, followed by the Conservatives with 18 seats. The Lib-Dems manage two seats and UKIP, receiving only 1% of the vote, have no MEPs at all.

On the same day as the European elections Nigel Farage aged 30, stands in the Eastleigh by-election in Hampshire getting just 952 (1.7%) of the votes. A traditional Conservative safe seat, it is taken by the Lib-Dems receiving 44.3% against the Conservative coming third with 24.7% of the votes.

The split over Europe in the Conservative party is very present. They lost a number of senior ministers over the previous decade as a direct result of European policy: Michael Heseltine (1986); Nigel Lawson (1989); Nicholas Ridley (1990); and Geoffrey Howe (1990). In the coming years there'll be many defections to other parties over disagreements on European issues. But what comes next is totally unexpected.

Nov. 1994 - Passing the European Finance Bill (EFB)

The Tory Rebels, as they are now called, are plotting their opposition to the forthcoming EFB vote on 28 November 1994 during the October Conservative Party Conference.

The EFB proposes increasing EU contribution payments by £75 million/year in 1995, rising to £250 million/year by the year 2000. This was negotiated back in December 1992, when the UK held the EEC Presidency headed up by John Major.

John Major makes it clear that this vote is an issue of confidence and carries a three-line whip. He also threatens that the consequence of not voting is losing the whip. On its second reading, Major wins the vote with a clear majority of 27. The bill to increase EU contributions passes.

Eight Tory Rebels abstain on a Labour amendment, which results in them having the whip withdrawn. A ninth rebel allegedly resigns the party whip of his own accord.

Major's reaction is unprecedented, after all, the eight MPs hadn't actually voted against the Government, they'd abstained, and the bill had passed with a comfortable majority. The action of withdrawing the whip en masse results in Major now presiding over a minority Government.

A month later right-wing Conservatives begin a campaign for the reinstatement of the Tory Rebels. The Conservative whip is eventually restored to all nine MPs on 24 April 1995.

November 1994 - Enter the Referendum Party

As John Major deals with party discord, businessman and billionaire Sir James Goldsmith launches the Referendum Party on 28 November 1994. This party only has one policy: to force an in-out referendum. It contests over 500 seats in the May 1997 general election and spends more on advertising than the Conservatives and Labour combined. They receive just under 3% of the votes and win no seats. So, what makes Sir James Goldsmith interesting? He is part of an elite that is questioning the motives of the EU. Long before it was fashionable, he argued that monetary union could not work without political union, but that would mean a transfer of sovereignty to Brussels, which no one in Europe had voted for. He says:

'The effects of a single currency go far beyond the economy. They would transform the political structure of Europe as well as the stability of its societies.'

'The true purpose of proposing a single currency is to force through the creation of a unitary state while pretending to promote a largely economic idea. It is yet another example of the Eurocrats acting by stealth so as to achieve their aim of a homogenized European union.'

Unfortunately, Goldsmith dies just two months after the May 1997 elections, resulting in the break-up of the party. Some supporters go on to create a Eurosceptic pressure group called the Democracy Movement, others join the newly formed UK Independence Party (UKIP).

Goldsmith's main achievement though, was getting mainstream newspapers to give more coverage to the Eurosceptic stance which influenced public opinion with regard to the Maastricht Treaty and matters of adopting the euro.

November 1994 - Court of Auditors report

The European Court of Auditors' report on the financial state of the EU alleges that 10% of the budget is lost due to fraud and waste. This draws attention to the most important weaknesses in relation to spending in East Central Europe, and to the failure of the European Parliament to enforce competitive tenders for its Brussels building programme.

MP Bill Cash (Tory Rebel) seizes on the report to argue that 'British tax payers were contributing to a bottomless fraudulent pit'. The Commission is quick to point out that the 482-page report is neither comprehensive nor balanced.

Nov. 1994 - Norway rejects joining the EU by 52.2%

June 1995 - John Major battles for party leadership

Critics of John Major doubt that he's capable of uniting the party over the issue of Europe. Major throws down the gauntlet during a press conference with the infamous words, 'Put up or shut up'. Conservative Eurosceptic MP John Redwood resigns as Secretary of State for Wales and challenges John Major for the position of Party Leader. Some big guns back him - Lord (Norman) Tebbit and former Chancellor, Norman Lamont. Redwood's campaign is based on his belief that Major is an electoral liability and the best chance for MPs to retain their seats lies in the appointment of a new leader. John Major announces his resignation as Party Leader on 22 June 1995 to face off against a single challenger.

As there are only two candidates the winner requires 50% of the votes plus a mandatory 15% more than their opponent - about 190 votes.

In the first ballot, Major receives 218 votes (66%) against Redwood's 89. Major has a Cabinet reshuffle, which unsurprisingly does not include Mr Redwood.

March 1996 - European Commission bans British beef

After Health Secretary Stephen Dorrell's speech in Parliament claiming there's a link between Creutzfeldt-Jakob disease and bovine spongiform encephalopathy (BSE or, more popularly, mad cow disease), the European Commission (EC) bans the export of British beef to Europe. Due to this action, British beef is then banned worldwide and by the end of 1997 over a million cattle in Britain have been destroyed.

In retaliation for the EU ban on beef exports, John Major announces on 21 May that the UK will veto all EU decisions that require unanimous support. Nigel Farage's first European Parliament speech is about beef, he says:

'Without the EU ban, Britain would have been able to exploit alternative markets and this crisis would not have arisen.'

'Now we have a classic demonstration that membership of the EU is bad for British business. It affirms my belief that it is about time my own country realises that our interests are best served by not being a member of this club.'

Later in 1996, Conservative Paymaster General David Heathcoat-Amory resigns, citing Major's refusal to rule out Britain's future membership of the single currency, and Lord McAlpine, a former Conservative party treasurer, defects to the Referendum Party.

John Major prorogues Parliament 19 days early

Major announces an election for 1 May 1997 as he presides over a minority Government (of -1) following the death of MP Iain Mills back in January.

John Major controversially prorogues parliament on 21 March (19 days earlier than it would normally be dissolved for an election) to avoid an embarrassing parliamentary debate on the cash-for-questions affair.

In a successful sting operation by The Sunday Times July 1994, journalists approach Conservative MPs asking them to submit questions to Parliament in exchange for cash payments. The Guardian later reports on two other Tory MPs who took bribes to table questions on behalf of Harrods tycoon Mohamed Al-Fayed. After these incidents Major sets up the Nolan Committee on Standards in Public Life.

The cash-for-questions scandal had been front page news three years earlier and the timing of Major's prorogation held up publication of a damning report and delayed a debate just prior to a general election - when the last thing you want is stories about Conservative MPs taking bribes. Whether or not that was his intention is debatable.

Years later, Sir John Major joins a court battle to reverse Boris Johnson's prorogation of Parliament over 9-12 September 2019, just four days before party conference season begins.

May 1997 - 'New Labour' wins a 179 seat majority

After rebranding the Party 'New Labour', the charismatic new Prime Minister Tony Blair aged just 43 ends 18 years of Labour Opposition. Labour wins 418 seats; the Liberal Democrats (led by Paddy Ashdown) double their position with 46 seats; the Conservatives are left with a mere 165 - a massive shift.

The Labour manifesto contains five main policies and talks a lot about Conservative broken promises. Blair promises a referendum on the EU single currency. Part of his campaign speech talks about EU reform:

'We will give Britain the leadership in Europe which Britain and Europe need. We will stand up for Britain's interests in Europe after the shambles of the last six years, but, more than that, we will lead a campaign for reform in Europe. Europe isn't working in the way this country and Europe need.'

CHAPTER FIVE

THE BLUNDER YEARS

May 1997 - Manifesto promises new life for Britain

Some key parts of the 1996 Labour manifesto that led to their landslide victory:

We will oppose a European federal suprastate.

Lead reform of the EU.
We have set out a detailed agenda for reform, leading from the front during the UK presidency in the first half of 1998.

Rapid completion of the single market.
We will open up markets to competition; pursue tough action against unfair state aid; and ensure proper enforcement of single market rules.

High priority for enlargement of the European Union.
To include the countries of central and eastern Europe and Cyprus.

Urgent reform of the Common Agricultural Policy.
It is costly, vulnerable to fraud and not geared to environmental protection. Enlargement and the World Trade talks in 1999 will make reform even more essential. We will seek a thorough overhaul of the Common Fisheries Policy to conserve our fish stocks in the long-term interests of the UK fishing industry.

Greater openness and democracy in EU institutions.
With open voting in the Council of Ministers and more effective scrutiny of the Commission by the European Parliament.

Retention of the national veto over key matters.
Matters of national interest, such as taxation, defence and security, immigration, decisions over the budget and future treaty changes.

Britain to sign the Social Chapter.
An empty chair at the negotiating table is disastrous for Britain. The Social Chapter is a framework under which legislative measures can be agreed. Only two measures have been agreed. The Social Chapter cannot be used to force the harmonisation of social security [which is higher in Germany for example] or tax legislation and it does not cost jobs. We will use our participation to promote employability and flexibility, not high social costs.

A referendum on adopting a single currency.

The manifesto states:

'Any decision about Britain joining the single currency must be determined by a hard-headed assessment of Britain's economic interests. Only Labour can be trusted to do this. But there are formidable obstacles in the way of Britain being in the first wave of membership if economic and monetary union (EMU) takes place on 1 January 1999 (actually launched in 1992). What is essential for the success of EMU is genuine convergence among the economies that take part, without any fudging of the rules. However, to exclude British membership of EMU forever would be to destroy any influence we have over a process which will affect us whether we are in or out. We must therefore play a full part in the debate to influence it in Britain's interests.'

'In any event, there are three preconditions which would have to be satisfied before Britain could join during the next Parliament: first, the Cabinet would have to agree; then Parliament; and finally, the people would have to say "Yes" in a referendum.'

> ## No such referendum ever takes place

After the sudden death of Labour leader John Smith in May 1994, Tony Blair is elected Leader of the Opposition, defeating John Prescott and Margaret Beckett. Straight away he rebrands the party, giving it the name 'New Labour'. Smith's cautious approach of keeping a low profile and banking on the unpopularity of the Conservatives to give Labour an election win is not Blair's style.

Blair was born into working-class surroundings in Edinburgh. The family moved to Adelaide, Australia, before his second birthday returning to the UK some four years later.

At nineteen he studies law at Oxford and graduates in 1975 with a second-class Honours BA in jurisprudence. A short time later he joins the Labour party and puts himself forward as a councillor in 1982 but isn't selected. He then runs in a by-election in the safe Conservative seat of Beaconsfield, and loses.

The Conservatives see an advantage in changing constituency boundaries, which creates the new constituency of Sedgefield, County Durham. A number of Labour MPs make a grab for the seat, but Blair approaches the local Labour branch and convinces the branch secretary to nominate him. Blair, aged 30, wins the seat in the 1983 election and receives his first front-bench appointment a year later as assistant Treasury spokesman. He continues on up through the ranks and becomes Shadow Home Secretary under John Smith before becoming Leader.

One of Blair's key moves is the decision not to let go of Thatcher's economic policies but to expand on them. Nationalization of everything that moves, a Labour cornerstone, is now off the agenda. Thatcherism had changed the very fabric of society, and things like privatization are no longer frowned upon - especially among those who had benefited from the purchase of a council house.

On the upside, Blair introduces the national minimum wage and national programmes to end poverty.

When Blair takes power in May 1997 net migration to the UK is about 48,000. A year later, it jumps to around 140,000 and never goes below 100,000 per year thereafter. People in EU countries have discovered the benefits of living in the UK.

A now, very pro-European Tony Blair very quickly delivers on his manifesto promise and signs Britain up to the Social Chapter on 18 June 1997.

June 1997 - John Major steps down

William Hague takes over as Conservative Party Leader at the age of 36. He beats two experienced Cabinet members, Kenneth Clarke (57) and Michael Howard (56). He must now resurrect a party that had suffered its worst ever defeat.

Just two years later Hague succeeds in beating Labour at the European Parliamentary elections winning 36 seats to Labour's 29.

July 1997 - Agenda 2000 tabled by EC

The Agenda 2000 programme, tabled by the EC, sets out a blueprint to establish a new financial framework in preparation for EU enlargement. The level of structural and cohesion funding is to be paired with proposed cuts of 20% in the cereal support price in the year 2000, a reduction of 30% in the beef intervention price between 2000 and 2002, and a 10% decline in the support price for milk. These cutbacks will take place against the backdrop of a new world trade agreement which will seek to eliminate export refunds. This is the first attempt to cut subsidies to farmers.

October 1997 - The Treaty of Amsterdam is signed

This is the first attempt to update the Maastricht Treaty and to prepare for the future accession of ten new member states. It takes two years of negotiations before all 12 States sign - the UK now adopts the Social Chapter.

The treaty also introduces the idea of a two-speed Europe, allowing countries that want to forge ahead with a closer union to do so.

The Schengen agreement later becomes law and gets rid of internal border checks for all member states - except for Britain and Ireland who opted out. Most importantly, it increases the Union's powers and removes some executive powers from the European Council and gives them to the Commission.

In the lead-up to the Treaty of Amsterdam four countries hold a referendum in preparation for joining the EU:

➢ Austria, June 1994, votes to join by 66.6% (82% turnout)

➢ Finland, October 1994, votes to join by 56.9%

➢ Åland Islands (Finland), Nov. 1994, votes to join by 73.6%

➢ Sweden, November 1994, votes to join by 52.3%.

Only two member states hold referendums to the ratification of the Treaty of Amsterdam:

➢ Ireland, May 1998, votes in favour by 61.7%

➢ Denmark, May 1998, votes in favour by 55.1% (76% TO).

There are referendums and EUphoria (sorry) among countries keen to join and member states keen to have them join.

30 October 1997 the UK gives the EU Council notice that it will not be adopting the single currency on 1 January 1999. It also reserves the right to adopt it at a later date.

The predecessor to the euro, known as the EMU, was a virtual currency only used for commercial and financial transactions. It had been adopted by 11 of the 15 member states. By 1 January 2002, 12 member states have adopted the euro as legal tender phasing out their own national currency.

Whereas Britain and Denmark opt out, Sweden refuses to meet the criteria, disallowing its implementation.

Corruption scandal forces the entire EC to resign

The European Commission helps shape the EU's overall strategy, proposes new laws and policies, monitors their implementation, and manages the budget and day-to-day business of the EU. It employs around 32,000 civil servants to carry out these duties.

On 15 July 1994, the European Council appoints Jacques Santer, ex-Prime Minister of Luxembourg, as President of the European Commission (known as the Santer Commission, 23 January 1995-15 March 1999). The selection of 20 committee members falls to the Commission President, under Maastricht Treaty rules which require only EU Parliamentary endorsement.

The Santer Commission's document entitled Agenda 2000, proposes a radical reform of the common agricultural policy (CAP), and to make structural funds more efficient as enlargement of the Union approaches.

The Commission is scrutinized by the European Parliament, who refuse to sign off their accounts for the 1996 financial year. Articles appear in German and Scandinavian newspapers about undue payments to certain MEPs.

In 1999 the entire European Union Executive Commission is forced to resign by the EU Parliament after a scathing report on corruption. The internal auditor of the Commission's financial control unit, Mr. Paul van Buitenen, discovers a series of irregularities with regard to payments of allowances.

He accuses the French EU Commissioner Édith Cresson of serious and repeated fraud, of falsifying contracts, of forging signatures and of embezzling EU funds. She hires René Berthelot, a dental surgeon and close friend, to be a highly paid EU adviser on HIV/Aids. Berthelot was later judged to be unqualified, and over two years had produced just 24 pages of notes of little or no value. In 2006, the European Court of Justice finds that Mrs. Cresson had acted in breach of her obligations as European Commissioner. Manuel Marin, the Spanish Commissioner, was also found guilty of fraud in relation to humanitarian aid. Jacques Santer does not remove either one of the Commissioners from their post despite being found guilty of fraud.

Other Commission members are now being investigated. At a meeting of the Commission they decide to all resign together. Too many skeletons?

Next comes the Prodi Commission, led by former Italian PM Romano Prodi (1999-2004). Four members of the Santer Commission, including ex-Labour Leader Neil Kinnock, are reappointed to the committee. The Amsterdam Treaty had increased the Commission's powers to such an extent that the press dubbed Prodi as being akin to the first EU Prime Minister.

The Barroso Commission follows (2004-2014).

Who is opting out of what?

To allow the EU agenda to move forward, countries are given the right to opt-out of parts of a treaty.. Once a member state is granted an opt-out it's permanent until that country decides to opt-in. This avoids an overall stalemate and creates a two-speed Europe. This is cherry picking you might say.

Examples of opt-outs include:

➢ Schengen Agreement: Ireland and the UK

➢ Economic and monetary union: Denmark and the UK

➢ Defence: Denmark

➢ EU Charter of Fundamental Rights: Poland and the UK

➢ Freedom, security and justice: Denmark, Ireland and the UK

Closer unification of member states is scheduled for the year 2020. Will all EU members then have to adopt the euro?

The UK and Denmark opt-outs exclude membership of the euro currency. A member state can decide to relinquish any of its opt-outs, but the EU can't currently force a country to surrender them.

As you see, the UK has opted-out of quite a few things.

April 1998 - Signing the Good Friday Agreement

There has been conflict in Ireland ever since Oliver Cromwell, Lord Protector of England, marched into Ireland in August 1649 to wage war against the Roman Catholics. (Cromwell, by the way, established the precedent that an English monarch requires consent from Parliament to rule, which still stands.)

The 1921 split that created the Irish Free State and a Northern Ireland with direct rule from Westminster caused more than a century of unrest between Britain and Ireland.

I remember scenes of violence on the television during the 1960s and 1970s as armed groups on both sides carried out deadly bombings in Britain and Northern Ireland. Margaret Thatcher's campaign manager and spokesman on Northern Ireland, Mr Airey Neave, was assassinated by an Irish National Liberation Army car bomb outside Westminster. Imprisoned members of the Irish Republican Army (IRA) went on hunger strike in a bid to get prisoner-of-war status, ten of them die. With Bloody Sundays and Bloody Fridays, it seemed like there would never be an end to the troubles.

The breakthrough comes on 31 August 1994, when the IRA declares a ceasefire and the bombings and shootings stop. This allows negotiations to open up that culminate in the IRA signing the Good Friday Agreement (The Belfast Agreement) at 5:30 pm on Friday 10 April 1998, ratified by referendums that put an end to the Northern Ireland conflict.

It is no doubt one of the most important documents created for achieving peace within the United Kingdom and the Republic of Ireland (ROI). Here is an extract from Article 1:

Two Governments:

(i) recognise the legitimacy of whatever choice is freely exercised by a majority of the people of Northern Ireland with regard to its status, whether they prefer to continue to support the Union with Great Britain or a sovereign united Ireland;

(ii) recognise that it is for the people of the island of Ireland alone, by agreement between the two parts respectively and without external impediment, to exercise their right of self-determination on the basis of consent, freely and concurrently given, North and South, to bring about a united Ireland, if that is their wish, accepting that this right must be achieved and exercised with and subject to the agreement and consent of a majority of the people of Northern Ireland;

(iii) acknowledge that while a substantial section of the people in Northern Ireland share the legitimate wish of a majority of the people of the island of Ireland for a united Ireland, the present wish of a majority of the people of Northern Ireland, freely exercised and legitimate, is to maintain the Union and accordingly, that Northern Ireland's status as part of the United Kingdom reflects and relies upon that wish; and that it would be wrong to make any change in the status of Northern Ireland save with the consent of a majority of its people;

The agreement creates the Northern Ireland Assembly to allow some self-rule. It is the start of devolution within the United Kingdom - later, Scotland and Wales get their own Parliaments. Although ongoing disagreements between the main parties cause the Northern Ireland Assembly to collapse in January 2017 the agreement still stands.

An open border between Northern Ireland and the ROI is an important part of the peace process to appease the IRA's goal of a united Ireland. Article 1 recognises the legitimacy of the desire for a united Ireland, while declaring that it can only be achieved through a referendum. Such a referendum would most likely fail as the majority of people in Northern Ireland are Protestants in favour of continued union with Great Britain.

When Northern Ireland and the ROI joined the European Single Market in 1992 checks on goods at the border are phased out and give the feeling of a single country. The 1998 GFA then de-escalates the conflict to a point where a militarized border is no longer necessary. This is the invisible, frictionless border that all now want to defend, although there is no specific mention of open borders in the GFA.

Tensions have not gone away, and people still live segregated lives, kids attend non-secular schools and play different sports. Fortunately, the riots, bomb blasts and sniper fire that have claimed the lives of some 3,600 people are a thing of the past. Anything that jeopardizes this fragile truce could mean the return of violence and killings that many would rather forget.

September 2000 - Danish euro referendum

Denmark, 28 September 2000, 53.2% against, turnout 87.6%

They'd opted out of the euro when signing the Maastricht Treaty, but could later chose to put it to the people. The turnout of over 87% is very high and the people send a clear message saying no to adopting the euro as their currency.

February 2001 - The Treaty of Nice is signed

To facilitate EU enlargement by a further ten states, adding 70 million people to its ranks, the Treaty of Nice agrees to limited institutional adaptations - especially on voting rules in Council and proposals to reduce the number of Commissioners.

The plan is for ten countries to join the EU in 2004: Poland, Hungary, Lithuania, Latvia, Estonia, Slovenia, Slovakia, Czech Republic, Malta and Cyprus. Membership of the EU would then be 25 countries with 456 million people.

The system in which all 12 member states have to agree unanimously leads to very watered-down policies. With 25+ states this would be even worse, so the Treaty of Nice calls for a qualified majority when voting (QMV).

This treaty is very much about a balance of power within the EU. Germany pushes to have more say, arguing that its 82 million inhabitants should give it more voting power than the UK, with only 60 million. The Netherlands with 15 million inhabitants has the same issue with regard to Belgium, with only 10 million. Brussels rejects the idea of having less power than its northern neighbour. This results in: Germany, France, the United Kingdom, and Italy getting 29 votes each; Spain and Poland getting 27 votes; and other countries getting progressively fewer votes depending on population size.

No single member can veto a proposal. A veto requires at least 62% of the Union's population. This means that a combination of the four 'big' states is enough to veto anything or a combination of Eastern bloc countries.

It is the same with the allocation of 732 seats for MEPs. Germany can elect 99 MEPs, France, the United Kingdom, and Italy get 72 each. Spain and Poland get 50 seats, the rest get progressively fewer seats according to population.

The treaty calls for enhanced competencies of the President of the EC, who now has to be elected by a qualified majority and be ratified by the European Parliament.

An Irish referendum in June 2001 rejects the Nice Treaty by 54%, but a second referendum in October 2002 passes it. Denmark and France also ratify it via referendums.

This treaty gives the EU permission to bring in new members, including Eastern Bloc countries, who will require financial aid for many years to come. A treaty driven mostly by Germany's Chancellor Helmut Kohl, who sees the benefits of having cheap production facilities and cheaper labour on his doorstep.

Labour Prime Minister Tony Blair doesn't see the need for a referendum. On the bill's third reading it is passed by 392 to 158 votes. More than 100 MPs don't bother to vote at all. Given Labour's huge majority the result is easy to foresee. Secretary of State Jack Straw opposes a referendum, citing:

> 'The idea to hold a referendum on the Nice Treaty is absurd and contradictory to British tradition.'
> Secretary of State Jack Straw

So, according to Jack Straw MP (Lab) there's a British 'tradition' of not giving the people a say on such matters.

Ratification by all other states happens without major difficulties and carried out via parliamentary procedure.

> **Treaty of Nice comes into force on 1 February 2003**

June 2001 - Labour wins election with 165 majority

Voter turnout is 12% down on the previous election. With just five fewer seats, Labour are in a great position to push policies through. They end their first-term promise to match the Conservatives on public spending. Gordon Brown, Chancellor of the Exchequer, now goes on a spending spree and increases budgets for the NHS, schools, and other public services.

William Hague has not managed to lift the Conservative Party out of the doldrums, they only win 165 seats. The party is deeply divided on the EU and perceived by the public as shifting too far to the right. After three months Hague resigns, and Tory rebel Iain Duncan Smith stands in as party leader.

This election sees two future Conservative Prime Ministers become new MPs: David Cameron and Boris Johnson.

January 2002 - The Euro (€) is cross-Europe currency

The UK, Denmark and Sweden remain outside the euro.

Referendums to join the EU held in these countries

With free money up for grabs, here's how the voting went:

➤ Malta, March 2003 - 53.6% in favour, turnout 90.9%

➤ Slovenia, March 2003 - 89.6% in favour, turnout 60.2%

➤ Hungary, April 2003 - 83.8% in favour, turnout 45.6%

➤ Lithuania, May 2003 - 91.9% in favour, turnout 63.4%

➤ Slovakia, May 2003 - 93.7% in favour, turnout 52.1%

➤ Poland, June 2003 - 77.5% in favour, turnout 58.9%

➤ Czech Rep., June 2003 - 77.3% in favour, turnout 55.2%

➤ Estonia, September 2003 - 66.8% in favour, turnout 64.1%

➤ Latvia, September 2003 - 67.5% in favour, turnout 71.5%

From Iraq war to the Chilcot report

Blair agrees to launch attacks on Iraq with the USA creating a legacy of regret that lessens his popularity. This is the last election to give any party a majority of more than 100 seats.

The Iraq Inquiry was announced in 2009 by Prime Minister Gordon Brown and published in 2016. The head of the inquiry, John Chilcot, said in presenting its findings: 'It is now clear that policy on Iraq was made on the basis of flawed intelligence and assessments. They were not challenged and they should have been.'

April 2003 - Ten states sign Treaty of Accession

The Treaty of Accession defines conditions for the ten new member states when they join the EU. The Maastricht Treaty says that all new members are obliged to adopt the euro. Only seven (Estonia, Cyprus, Latvia, Lithuania, Malta, Slovenia, Slovakia) qualify to join the eurozone (the group name for members that adopt the euro), three don't.

The Czech Republic, Hungary and Poland don't meet the Maastricht criteria for joining the eurozone nor the EU, but are nevertheless allowed in - by 2022 there is still no target date for them to adopt the euro.

Annual opinion polls in the Czech Republic over the last ten years show that a referendum would likely end in the euro being rejected by at least 60% of the population.

Sept. 2003 - Swedish referendum says no to euro (€)

➢ Sweden, September 2003, 55.9% against, turnout 82.6%

June 2004 - An 'EC Constitution' is proposed

The European Commission under Romano Prodi starts the 'Penelope Project' in 2001. This is a plan to create a single constitution to replace all existing treaties and to define more clearly who does what in the EU. Sold by the EC as an innocent 'tidying-up exercise' to make the EU more workable, it is undoubtedly a massive grab for power.

Critics of the Penelope Project see it as an attempt to give more powers to the Commission relative to Parliament and Council. The final draft of the 'EU Constitutional Treaty' includes creating the new position of President of the EU.

Under the 'EU Constitutional Treaty', the EU would become a sovereign entity with a governing body in its own right. The European Court of Justice would become the EU Supreme Court. The big winners would be MEPs, who could fast track constitutional change as referendum failures in member states during ratification would not veto a policy, given the introduction of qualified majority voting (QMV).

QMV means, 'at least 55% of the members of the Council, comprising at least fifteen of them and representing member states making at least 65% of the population of the Union'.

In my opinion, the ramifications of the Penelope Project are more far-reaching than I have described, as I believe it was an attempt to create a federal state. Step by step, power would shift from member states as Parliament and Council become QMV-driven and more powerful. It was the concept of QMV that prompted Margaret Thatcher's 'no, no, no' speech.

The EU Constitutional Treaty which establishes an 'EU Constitution' is adopted by the European Council on 18 June 2004, signed in Rome on 29 October 2004 by all representatives of the 25 member states of the EU. It's sent to be ratified by all 25 states, either by referendum or parliamentary procedure. You might think, it's a done deal.

The treaty is passed overwhelmingly by 16 member states, the number of parliamentarians against it are in the single digits. It's written into the treaties of Bulgaria and Romania so when they join in 2005, automatically agree to the terms.

May 2005, France holds a referendum where 54.68% vote against the treaty, rejecting the EU Constitutional Treaty.

Tony Blair is asked, if he thinks the treaty is dead or is he still keeping on his promise to have a referendum:

'If there is a constitutional treaty, I mean, let me make it clear as I've said many times before, if there's a constitutional treaty to vote upon, we will have a vote in Britain before ratifying it. But, I think, now you've got to see what happens in the Dutch referendum in a couple of days...'

Two days later the Netherlands referendum shows a

worse result, with 61.54% of voters against ratifying the EU Constitutional Treaty. On the basis of these results, seven countries, including the UK, cancel planned referendums.

How Blair deals with the EU Constitutional Treaty

20 April 2004 - Tony Blair announces his intention to hold a referendum, without giving any date. No less than eight other member states announce they will also hold referendums on the EU Constitutional Treaty. In view of the UK Government's massive majority, and to not go against a British 'tradition', why on earth would they want a referendum?

The new Labour Foreign Secretary, Jack Straw, is the driving force for a referendum within the Cabinet (yes, the same Jack Straw). He says the vote would have 'wider implications' for Britain's relationship with Europe but would not be a choice between being 'in or out'. He insists that Tony Blair would not have to resign if he lost.

Tony Blair says in Parliament:

'It is time to resolve once and for all whether this country, Britain, wants to be at the centre and heart of European decision-making or not. Time to decide whether our destiny lies as a leading partner and ally in Europe or on its margins. Let the issue be put and let the battle be joined.'

He says the choice would become very clear as the debate continued - between Britain playing its full part in the EU or going down a road favoured by the Conservatives, which would 'change fundamentally' its relationship with Europe.

Take this speech in context of what we now know, that Blair had ambitions to become the first permanent EU President.

I can only imagine that the Labour Cabinet and eight other member states realized that this was a treaty of such magnitude, it would change their constitution to such a degree that they had to protect themselves from any negative consequences, and only a referendum could do that.

Eight other EU states, six of which had never had an EU referendum before, were also planning to give the people a voice for the first time.

April 2004 - Tony Blair on migration

Immigration is becoming a big issue with the general public after scandals about migrant abuse of the system touch on the British sense of genuine unfairness. This, coupled with a looming election, inspire Tony Blair to make a speech outlining the Government's immigration strategy.

During the ten years of Tony Blair's tenure, over two million more migrants than the Government had expected settle in Britain. As there is no clear policy on integration new arrivals tend to live in communities of their own kind. Blair does not see the mass influx of people as an issue. He dismisses as 'racist' the Tory warnings about Third World economic migrants entering Britain as tourists and then claiming asylum. The Home Office reckons that in 1995 asylum-seekers had claimed more than £200 million in benefits - yet only 5% were genuine refugees. However, Blair does recognize a problem with bogus asylum seekers, and it becomes an election issue after 1999. He converts over 350,000 asylum-seekers into economic migrants, gives them work permits, and rights to social benefits. This gives an impression that the UK is a soft touch, which results in thousands of illegal immigrants heading over.

May 2005 - Labour wins an historic third term

Not by as large a majority as four years earlier, but winning 355 seats. The Conservatives with 198 and the Liberal Democrats 62, leaving Labour with a comfortable majority.

Every party's manifesto for the 2005 election offers a referendum on the EU Constitutional Treaty.

Labour says: 'We will put it (the Constitutional Treaty) to the British people in a referendum and campaign wholeheartedly for a "Yes" vote to keep Britain a leading nation in Europe.'

The Labour manifesto says the EU Constitutional Treaty sets out what the EU can and cannot do; strengthens the voice of national parliaments and governments in EU affairs; and ensures that Britain keeps control of key national interests like foreign policy, taxation, social security, and defence.

The Conservative view is: 'We oppose the EU Constitutional Treaty and will give the people the chance to reject its provisions in a referendum within six months of the general election.'

The Lib-Dems are 'clear in our support for the constitution, which we believe is in Britain's interest - but ratification must be subject to a referendum of the British people'.

> **For all three major parties to be this much in favour of a referendum, it must be really important!**

The EU Constitutional Treaty is set aside

It all falls apart as European leaders announce plans to set aside the EU Constitutional Treaty for a 'period of reflection' because the negative results of the Dutch and French referendums that hinder ratification, which requires all member states to sign up to the treaty.

This is not the end of the EU Constitutional Treaty -

by any means!

Romano Prodi steps down as EC President in October 2004 and is replaced by José Manuel Barroso in November 2004.

The Barroso Commission revives the EU Constitutional Treaty and begins to mull over ways to make it acceptable. A State of the Union Address by Barroso in 2012 openly says: 'We will need to move towards a federation of nation states.'

July-December 2005 - UK EU Presidency

With Tony Blair as President of the Council of the EU for the next six months, Britain could push policy in her favour.
In the final month of his presidency, Tony Blair agrees to give up 20% (£7 billion per year) of Britain's rebate (as negotiated by Margaret Thatcher). These are extra funds the EU needs to help prop up failing economies, but they are listed as modernization funds for the eight east European newcomers - to the tune of €862 billion of taxpayers' money for 2007-2013. However, for the first time the deal does raise France's contribution to be equal to Britain's.

Nigel Farage, at the European Parliament on 20 December 2005, can hardly contain himself as he aims a speech at the blunders of Tony Blair. He said that Mr Blair had given the EU billions for "nothing in return".

'Why should British taxpayers pay for new sewers in Budapest, for a new underground system in Warsaw when our own public services are crumbling in London'

'Why should we pay a penny piece into an organisation whose accounts have not been signed by the auditors for the last 11 years in a row?'

An angry Tony Blair attacks Farage defending the €862bn (£586bn) EU budget which sees Britain give up £7bn of its rebate for the period 2007-13 saying, 'This is the year 2005, not 1945. We are not fighting each other any more.'

Dec. 2005 - Cameron becomes Conservative Leader

After their defeat in the May 2005 elections, Michael Howard steps down and David Cameron becomes Leader of the Conservative Party on 6 December 2005.

EU Constitutional Treaty is revived by Amato Group

Millions of euros spent creating an EU Constitutional Treaty that was defeated by Dutch and French referendums, but the Commission is not going to be deterred.

Now driven by the Barroso Commission, there's an unofficial meeting on 30 September 2006 in Rome. As part of the 'reflection period' a group of 16 'wise men' - consisting of MEPs, former prime ministers, and members of the EC - sit down to consider the next course of action to revive the EU Constitutional Treaty.

These 'wise men' include: Costas Simitis, former prime minister of Greece; Dominique Strauss-Kahn, Managing Director of the International Monetary Fund (IMF); Otto Schily, former German Interior Minister accused of receiving money to lobby for the prosecution in Austria of Rakhat Aliyev in 2015; Chris Patten, British Lord, European Commissioner and the last Governor of Hong Kong; they are led by the former Italian PM Giuliano Amato, hence the name, Amato Group.

They decide that the best way forward is to take the parts of the EU Constitutional Treaty that nobody objects to and dress it up as a completely new treaty. Those parts that nobody wants will be tabled as lots of amendments to the Treaty of Rome and the Maastricht Treaty.

At the end of 2007, the Amato Group change the name from 'EU Constitutional Treaty' to something far less threatening. As the place of signing is Barroso's home town, the EU Constitutional Treaty now becomes the 'Lisbon Treaty'.

Sept. 2006 - Group 'Better Off Out' launched

A non-party campaign brings together prominent people from both sides of the House as the 'Better Off Out' group. Their only aim is the UK's withdrawal from the EU. Supporters include Lord Tebbit, former DUP leader Ian Paisley, MP Peter Bone (Con), MP David Davies (Con), and Christopher Gill.

September 2006 - Nigel Farage elected UKIP Leader

On 12 September 2006 Nigel Farage is elected Leader of the UK Independence party, replacing Roger Knapman.

Nigel Farage left the Conservative Party in 1992 as a result of John Major signing the Maastricht Treaty. He becomes a founding member of UKIP in 1994 and MEP for South East England in the 1999 European Parliament elections.

Farage has running battles with EC President José Manuel Barroso from 2004. In 2005 Farage tables a vote of no confidence, accusing Barroso of misconduct for taking a vacation on a tycoon's luxury yacht. The motion is denounced by all major political groups in the legislature, but they called for greater transparency of the EU institutions.

'Europe is too secretive and too opaque, too many decisions taken behind closed doors,' said Graham Watson, leader of the Liberal Democrats in the Parliament.

May 2007 - Blair announces stepping down as PM

Blair's popularity never recovered after instigating the Iraq war based on false information from Germany about weapons of mass destruction, and his party see him as an electoral liability. On the tenth anniversary of the general election that swept him to power he announces his departure and endorses Gordon Brown as his successor. Blair, had made it clear in 2004 that he had no intention of standing for a fourth term as leader. In an interview 2006 with the Australian Broadcasting Corporation he admitted that his move may have destabilised his position in the Labour Party which left him open to calls for him to go, saying, 'I shouldn't have said I planned to quit.'

Tony Blair's last PMQs on 27 June 2007. The question from Sir Nicholas Winterton (Con) (at 24 minutes) calls for a referendum, citing the new Treaty (of Lisbon), which is, in substance, the old discredited EU Constitutional Treaty.

Blair finishes his PMQs with: 'Parliament is still the arena that sets the heart beating a little faster and if it is on occasions the place of low skulduggery, it is more often the place for the pursuit of noble causes.'

Brown's only contender for PM is MP John McDonnel, but he fails to get enough nominations for a place on the ballot and concedes defeat. On 24 June 2007 Gordon Brown is declared the new Labour Leader to replace the increasingly unpopular Tony Blair. As with John Major in his first term, Brown is not leader through the democratic process of the British electorate but through selection by a Labour party vote.

Signing the Lisbon Treaty

Before the Lisbon Treaty is signed, speculation is rife as to who will become the first European president as proposed in this new treaty. If the Irish back the treaty on 2 October 2009, EU leaders would decide on who will get the presidency during a summit at the end of the month.

The role of president is to create 'cohesion and consensus' among members states, 'drive forward' the EU's programs, and be the representative of the Union on issues concerning its common foreign and security policy. The office of the EU president will replace the current tradition of the rotating presidency, which sees a different member state taking over summit organizing responsibilities every six months.

Tony Blair has high hopes of becoming the first president of the EU with backing from the British government, although the former PM has not yet formally declared his candidacy. Britain's Europe Minister Lady Glenys Kinnock, in Strasbourg for the opening session of the new European parliament explains: 'I am sure they would not do it without asking him. The UK government is supporting Blair's candidature for president of the council. Blair is seen by many as someone who has the strength of character'... 'and he would be someone who would have this role and step into it with a lot of respect and I think would be generally welcomed.'

Britain's bid to promote Tony Blair as a candidate to become the first ever President of the European Union is met with unexpectedly vocal opposition in a number of European capital cities. Swedish PM Reinfeldt, whose country is to take the helm as President in June says, 'Small and medium-sized countries are less interested in having a strong leader.'

Back in April 2008, the terms of the new President were discussed at a secret „working dinner" between Jose Manuel Barroso, the European Commission president, and EU ambassadors, the Telegraph reported.

Conservatives and William Hague, the shadow Foreign Secretary, attacks the talks, held before the EU treaty has been fully debated and ratified at Westminster by giving a statement to the Telegraph: 'This shows how deeply undemocratic this whole process is. Crucial questions about the EU are being decided and Parliament, let alone the British people, is being kept in the dark. Ministers must now come clean about what they've been up to as the treaty is scrutinised in the Lords.'

'EU politicians claim that the Lisbon Treaty will make the EU more transparent and accessible to voters, but this latest example of secretive horse-trading shows that if it ever does come into force it will be business as usual in Brussels,' says Paul Stephenson, spokesman for Open Europe.

Tony Blair loses the bid to Herman Van Rompuy, the centre-right Belgian ex-prime minister. In a 2012 speech to the Council for the Future of Europe, Tony Blair makes the suggestion: 'Out of this European crisis can come the opportunity finally to achieve a model of European integration that is sustainable. A Europe wide election for the Presidency is the most direct way to involve the public.' Blair goes on to say, 'An election for a big post held by one person - that people can understand. The problem with the European Parliament is that though clearly democratically elected, my experience is people don't feel close to their MEPs. I can't see any new political settlement being acceptable without direct popular consent through referendums. The present situation is the most serious to have faced the EU since its inception, and as we speak, the crisis persists.'

In response, Nigel Farage said: 'This is the man who would sell his country for the bauble of EU office. The ideas contained in Blair's speech do however show, that even he is giving up on his old dream of Britain being at the heart of Europe...'

December 2007 - Lisbon Treaty signed

The Lisbon Treaty is signed by all 27 EU members, which starts the process of ratification, either by referendum or by parliamentary vote.

The Lisbon Treaty replaces the rejected EU Constitutional Treaty which had compelled nine countries to hold a referendum, given its far-reaching consequences on the constitutions of all 27 member states. This treaty keeps most of the old content but gives up any reference to the word 'constitution', saying it is only amending the Maastricht Treaty (1992) and the Treaty of Rome (1957) - 300 pages of amendments to 3,000 other pages of treaties. Nobody reads it, and nobody understands it!

I find statements from the EU such as, 'The Lisbon Treaty would give the European and national parliaments a bigger role in the decision-making process, and thus raise the EU's democratic profile', disconcerting. Does this mean abolishing referendums in favour of EU parliamentary votes?

As we now know, it's still a requirement that ALL EU member states ratify a treaty before it can become law - either by holding a referendum or by parliamentary consent.

> **Having learnt the lesson, that referendums just get in the way of EU democracy, 26 member states decide not to hold one.**

Only Ireland prepares to hold a referendum, so an...

Amendment to nullify the Irish referendum is tabled

In Strasbourg on 20 February 2008, the same day the EU Parliament will approve the Lisbon Treaty, a debate is held on the Corbett-de Vigo Report, proposing amendments to be voted on before the whole treaty is put to the vote.

To pre-empt a negative result from Ireland's referendum, amendment 32 asks that the European Parliament **'undertake to respect the outcome of the referendum in Ireland'.** In other words, will the EU Parliament respect the result of the forthcoming Irish referendum on the Lisbon Treaty?

> **The amendment to respect the Irish referendum is rejected by 499 votes to 129, - 33 abstain**

Even the Irish MEP - Proinsias de Rossa - votes not to respect his own country's referendum.

> *This one action of the EU Parliament nullifies a legitimate referendum, demonstrating how the EU's democratic profile can be raised.*

After the final vote on the Lisbon Treaty - 525 to 115 against, 29 abstentions - Hans-Gert Poettering, the President of the European Parliament, ends the ceremony saying:

'A vast majority of you have voted in favour of the Lisbon Treaty. This is an expression of the free will of the people you represent (except the people were not asked). I'd like to congratulate you on this convincing result.' He goes on;
'This European Parliament represents the people of Europe, this treaty gives the European Union the ability to function

properly and this treaty gives it more democracy. And we defend the common values of Europe and (referring to a few protesting MEPs) we shall never allow loud noise to override sensible arguments.'

The European Parliament sent a clear message to the Irish people that in their quest to ratify this treaty at any cost, they don't care what others have to say. A fine example of European democracy.

June 2008 - Irish hold a referendum on Lisbon Treaty

Ireland's constitution says that amendments can only be decided upon and ratified by the people. Amongst the 27 member states it's the only referendum held and the people say no to signing it.

➢ Ireland, June 2008, vote against by 53.4% (53.1% turnout)

Respect the Irish vote campaign is started

A campaign is started to 'Respect the Irish Vote' as Ireland decides to run a second referendum. During the debate, one phrase kept coming up from MEPs: 'We respect the vote of Ireland' (although they had just voted not to respect it). Re-running a referendum is a denial of democracy. It's no different to a defeated government re-running a general election in the hope that the voters will change their mind. Past behaviour of a parliament is a good indicator of its future behaviour. MEPs from Germany, Italy, France, and so on decided that the will of the Irish people should be annulled by a vote in the EU Parliament. Am I the only one who shudders at the consequences of this?

Sure there's uproar, but compared to how Sinn Féin would have reacted if the UK had done this, the response is mild.

What do you think would happen if the UK Parliament held a referendum, didn't like the result, then passed a bill in Parliament for 'more democratic accountability to respect the outcome of the referendum - aye or nay?' and then voted by 80% for no. Take a moment to consider how big and how violent the protests would be.

October 2009 - Ireland holds a second referendum

The pretext is that Government had renegotiated the terms of the treaty, so were presenting it to the Irish people to ask if Government could ratify it.

➢ Ireland, Oct. 2009 votes in favour by 67.1% (59.0% turnout)

The referendum asks to amend the Constitution of Ireland to permit the state to ratify the Treaty of Lisbon. This is not the same as asking if they agree with the treaty.

Jeremy Corbyn - ,A European empire of the 21st century'

Mr Corbyn is a lifelong Eurosceptic who voted for Britain to leave the European Community in 1975. Corbyn also opposed the ratification of the Maastricht Treaty in 1993, saying: „... the whole basis of the Maastricht Treaty is the establishment of a European central bank which is staffed by bankers, independent of national Governments and national economic policies, and whose sole policy is the maintenance of price stability. '

Speaking at a rally prior to the 2009 Irish referendum on whether to approve the Lisbon Treaty, which paved the way for more EU integration, Mr Corbyn, a backbencher MP, says, 'Under the terms of the Lisbon Treaty, Europe will become subservient to the wishes of Nato and the aims of Nato.... What it does is create this military machine, this military Frankenstein, which will be so damaging to all of us.'

France and Denmark should have held referendums

France and Denmark, whose constitutions also require a referendum, and who both voted down the EU Constitutional Treaty, are silenced.

February 2008, the French Parliament votes to amend the French Constitution to allow the Assemblée Nationale and the Senate to ratify the Lisbon Treaty.

Mr Nicolas Sarkozy reassures French voters that this is a mini treaty, with the constitutional aspects of the old EU Constitutional Treaty stripped out.

In Denmark, Prime Minister Anders Fogh Rasmussen decides alone not to hold a referendum on the Lisbon Treaty, leaving it for MPs to ratify. The treaty passes by 90 votes in favour and 25 against, 64 MPs out of the 179-seat parliament abstain. The Danish media portray Rasmussen as a candidate for President of the European Council if the Lisbon Treaty comes into force.

A class action lawsuit is filed in 2009 by 34 people who argue that because the treaty affects Danish sovereignty on a number of issues, it should have been submitted to a referendum. On 15 June 2012 Denmark's High Court finds that the country's Government is not obliged to hold a referendum before signing the Lisbon Treaty.

> **Only Ireland hold a referendum on the Lisbon Treaty**

How does the UK deal with ratification?

Jan. 2008 - Cameron pledges poll on Lisbon Treaty

Right from the start, just weeks after Gordon Brown signs the Lisbon Treaty, Opposition Leader David Cameron makes a bold statement. If the Tories win the next election, he promises to hold a referendum on the Lisbon Treaty, if it hasn't already been ratified. He says;

'As soon as we have an election, the sooner we can have a referendum'. He goes on to say,

'Why do we need a Referendum?'

'I think, when our Parliament is giving up powers, is passing powers to someone else, they should ask us first, the people, in a referendum'.

Gordon Brown's Labour Government believes a referendum isn't necessary because he's secured opt-outs and most changes made by the treaty are minor or procedural. Government's motion to ratify the Lisbon Treaty passes on 21 January 2008 by 362 to 224 votes. Royal assent is granted on 19 June 2008.

This Act doesn't actually ratify the treaty; it merely adds it to the treaties listed in the European Communities Act 1972. Ratification only takes place when Government deposits the ratification documents in Rome on 16 July 2008.

January 2008 - Black Monday

The Dow Jones falls by 12.8%. This is followed by Black Tuesday, when the Dow falls a further 30.57 points.

March 2008 - The Tories table a referendum motion

Although the House passed a motion to ratify the Lisbon Treaty back in January, the Tory Opposition tables an amendment calling for a vote on 5 March to allow a public referendum. They also support Ian Davidson (Labour backbencher), who additionally wants an in-out referendum on EU membership.

Cameron appeals to the Liberal Democrats to support a vote against their leader Nick Clegg, in a final push to secure a referendum on the Lisbon Treaty.

'Every political party promised one at the last election and only the Conservative Party is sticking to its pledge and campaigning for that referendum.' Mr Cameron went on, 'Voters would feel desperately let down if their MPs failed to honour previous election promises to give the people a say.'

Clegg, a strong pro-European, causes a rift in his party saying that the public should be granted an in-out vote. He argued that a vote on the Lisbon Treaty was unnecessary as it didn't make any significant constitutional changes.

> **British MPs reject the motion to holding a referendum to ratify the Lisbon Treaty.**

The House of Commons turn down the amendment by 311 votes to 248. Three Liberal Democrat frontbenchers Alistair Carmichael, Tim Farron and David Heath - resign after defying the party's order to abstain on the referendum vote.

MP Bill Cash's (Con) attempt on 17 June 2008 for a judicial review is rejected by the High Court, which confirmed that UK ratification without a referendum is legal. The judge rejected the claim on the grounds that it is for Parliament rather than the courts to decide whether a bill should pass, and that Cash was trying to 'pursue a political agenda through the court'.

THE BOTTOM LINE

This means that Parliament's decision to ratify the treaty back in January stands. On 16 July 2008 the UK is the first country after the Irish 'No' referendum to deposit its instrument of ratification in Rome.

The Lisbon Treaty says that if more than one million citizens from a representative number of member states (15) petition the Commission, then it should consider the request. But it does not have to act. And the petition can only relate to the proper implementation of EU treaties, not to something people might object to in the treaties. In practice, this will have little impact on the workings of the EU. How is anyone going to bring together one million citizens from 15 states?

Article 50

Article 50 is one of 358 clauses in the Lisbon Treaty. Ironically, it was drafted by the Scottish cross-bench peer and former diplomat Lord Kerr of Kinlochard. It outlines the steps a country needs to take in order to leave the EU voluntarily. Invoking Article 50 kick-starts the formal exit process by serving official notice of an intention to leave the EU.

The author of Article 50, that Scottish peer, hadn't originally seen it as necessary and says in November 2016: 'If you stopped paying the bills and you stopped turning up at the meetings, in due course your friends would notice that you seemed to have left.' He did think Article 50 could be useful in the event of a coup: 'I thought that at that point the dictator in question might be so cross that he'd say "right, I'm off" and it would be good to have a procedure under which he could leave.' He makes it sound so easy.

Article 50 states:

1. Any Member State may decide to withdraw from the Union in accordance with its own constitutional requirements.

2. A member state which decides to withdraw shall notify the European Council of its intention. In light of the guidelines provided by the European Council, the Union shall negotiate and conclude an agreement with that state, setting out the arrangements for its withdrawal, taking account of the framework for its future relationship with the Union. That agreement shall be negotiated in accordance with Article 218(3) of the Treaty on the Functioning of the European Union. It shall be concluded on behalf of the Union by the Council, acting by a qualified majority, after obtaining the consent of the European Parliament.

3. The treaties shall cease to apply to the state in question from the date of entry into force of the withdrawal agreement or, failing that, two years after the notification referred to in paragraph 2, unless the European Council, in agreement with the member state concerned, unanimously decides to extend this period.

a. For the purposes of paragraphs 2 and 3, the member of the European Council or of the Council representing the withdrawing member state shall not participate in the discussions of the European Council or Council or in decisions concerning it. A qualified majority shall be defined in accordance with Article 238(3)(b) of the treaty on the Functioning of the European Union.

b. If a State which has withdrawn from the Union asks to re-join, its request shall be subject to the procedure referred to in Article 49 (which means starting from scratch and re-applying).

June 2009 - European Parliament elections

To say there is apathy in the UK, is an understatement with only 34.3% of the population bothering to turn up to vote. The Lib-Dems get 13.3%, the Labour Party gets 15.7% and UKIP gets 16.5% of votes. The Conservatives win with 27.7%.

UKIP has an in-out referendum on UK membership of the EU at the heart of its programme.

November 2009 - Cameron: no hope of referendum

In an interview David Cameron says: 'The Lisbon Treaty has now been ratified by every one of the 27 member states of the European Union, and our campaign for a referendum on the Lisbon Treaty is therefore over.'

'Why? Because it is no longer a treaty: it is being incorporated into the law of the European Union. Next week, the new posts that the Lisbon Treaty creates - a President and a Foreign Minister - will be filled.'

Cameron claims the 'betrayal' was the fault of Labour and the Liberal Democrats and promises that such a situation will never happen again. If the Conservatives are elected, he'd change the law so that a referendum must be held before any further powers are passed to the European Union.
'This is not a treaty that Britain wanted or needed,' said Cameron. 'It's a treaty Gordon Brown was so ashamed of he had to sign it in a room all on his own.' he added, in reference to Prime Minister Gordon Brown's notorious late arrival at the signing ceremony in Lisbon the previous year.

The French accuse the Conservatives of 'castrating' Britain's position within the EU by adopting an 'autistic' approach that would take Britain off the radar. The angry exchange comes after the Tories hint that if they win the election, they would strengthen British sovereignty and repatriate a series of powers over social and employment legislation.

1 December 2009 - The Treaty of Lisbon becomes law

April 2010 - Lib-Dems offer conditional referendum

In preparation for the general election on 6 May 2010, Nick Clegg the leader of the Liberal Democrats pledges to hold an in-out referendum should there be a 'fundamental change' in the EU's treaty arrangements. A promise coming from a party that's never won more than 62 seats is not much of a promise and is hardly likely to come to fruition.

There was an election debate with Gordon Brown going head to head with David Cameron and Nick Clegg on 15 April 2010. Not one of these party leaders had led a general election campaign before. The very first question of the debate is on immigration policy, which highlights how important this subject is going to be in the coming years.

May 2010 - Cameron narrowly wins general election

After 13 years of a Labour Government, David Cameron's Conservative party scrapes over the line with just enough seats to form a minority Government. The real winner, and the one holding all the cards, is Nick Clegg (Lib-Dems).

Was Gordon Brown ever really electable against the charismatic David Cameron?

Although the Conservatives win most seats, they are just 20 short of the 326 seats needed to form a Government. This is only the second time since World War II that an election returns a hung parliament.

If Clegg decides to form a coalition with the Labour Party, then Gordon Brown will have another term as prime minister. The battle is on as old enemies hold talks over five days.

CHAPTER SIX

DAVID AND
GOLIATH

May 2010 - David Cameron becomes prime minister

On 11 May 2010, following Gordon Brown's resignation, David Cameron is forced to form the first coalition Government since World War II. He appoints the Leader of the Liberal Democrats, Nick Clegg, as Deputy Prime Minister.

The youngest UK Prime Minster since the 1810s inherits a country that is nearly bankrupt, again. The outgoing Labour Chief Secretary Liam Byrne left a note to the Treasury:

'Dear Chief Secretary I'm afraid there is no money.
Kind regards – and good luck! Liam.'

The note provoked widespread fury. A record £163billion annual borrowing deficit and £777billion national debt was left by Gordon Brown's defeated Labour administration.

David Cameron, born 9 October 1966, was brought up in an upper-middle-class family. This gave him the advantage of attending the same schools as royalty. From Eton College, Berkshire, he went on to the University of Oxford. At Oxford he was a member of a student dining society called the Bullingdon Club where he met and became friends with Boris Johnson. At the age of 18, he took time out to work as a researcher for the Lewes MP Tim Rathbone, which gave him the chance to sit in on debates in the House of Commons.

Cameron joined the Conservative Research Department in September 1988 and works his way up the ranks. He briefs John Major for PMQs and becomes head of the political section. He is pipped at the post for the position of Political Secretary to the Prime Minister but is responsible for briefing John Major before press conferences during the 1992 general election. The success of the campaign speaks for itself. Cameron is Special Adviser to the Chancellor of the Exchequer, Norman Lamont, during Black Wednesday and when sterling left the ERM. Cameron also had the task of informing the press of Lamont's resignation.

With a growing ambition to step into the political arena, Cameron puts his name on the Conservative Central Office list of prospective parliamentary candidates, September 1993.

He leaves politics to take a position as Director of Corporate Affairs at Carlton Communications, which produces weekday television among other things but leaves himself open to stand as a candidate should a Conservative seat become available.

For the second time he resigns his job to run for Parliament and wins the seat for Witney, Oxfordshire, to enter the House of Commons for the first time in June 2001, as Tony Blair starts his second term as Prime Minister. Due to his knowledge of the inner workings of Parliament he serves as a member of the Commons Home Affairs Select Committee, a senior position for a newly elected MP. He steadily climbs the ranks of the Conservative Party and announces his candidacy for the leadership position when Michael Howard steps down 2005.

Aged only 39, and with a little over four years' experience as an MP, he doesn't get much support from colleagues in the House. Cameron is considered the outsider against such seasoned politicians as David Davis, until his speech at the Conservative Party Conference in Blackpool, October 2005. The speech is so well received it puts him in the running for prime minister.

In the first ballot David Davis gets 62 votes, Cameron comes second with 56. Liam Fox's 42 and Kenneth Clarke's 38 votes give an indication of where the race is going.

In the second ballot on 20 October 2005 Cameron gets 90 votes and Davis gets 57. Then it goes to the entire party membership and Cameron gets twice as many votes, which makes him Leader of the Conservative Party (in opposition) on 6 December 2005.

May 2010 - Greece gets a €310 billion bailout

Greece's national sport is tax evasion, and corruption is rife. The retirement age is 45 and 25% of the population work directly for the Government (10% is the norm elsewhere). The Government refuses to collect taxes from their biggest industry - shipping, or from the biggest land owner giving away an income of 20 million euros each year. What a plan! How could something so well thought out, go so wrong?

After joining the EEC in 1981, Greece steadily goes further into bankruptcy and hides it well - until the financial debt crisis 2010 reveals their skulduggery. The Greek Government lied to gain access to the Common Market by falsifying accounts to give the impression they actually had an economy. In reality, Greece never met the criteria for joining the EU nor the requirements to join the eurozone.

So, what's the penalty for lying to the EU over so many years?

By 2019 Greece was given bailout funds worth €310 billion, but the Greek Government refuses to say what they're doing with the money.

One newspaper writes: 'The combined total of Greece's bailout is bigger than Hong Kong's economy.' Angela Merkel hands over €914 million of German taxpayers' money, but the people of Greece are up in arms when they find out it's a loan and call the Germans Nazis. The people of Greece are not broke, just the Government is.

THE BOTTOM LINE

A simple quick guide to the Greek bailout.
Did anyone do the maths?

➢ Total bailout money: €310,000,000,000

➢ Total population: 10,770,000

➢ Cash per head: €28,783

The German Chancellor Angela Merkel is blamed for the tough public spending cuts that follow bailouts from the EU and IMF.

Merkel justifies her decision to hold back approval of the bailout package until Germany could be absolutely sure Greece had met all of the preconditions. She said, 'Without sufficient consideration to preconditions, the expectations of other deeply indebted members of the eurozone would be that they would quickly receive help without implementing their own consolidation efforts would have risen.'

Merkel expresses her confidence in Athens to keep to its word, 'I trust that my Greek counterpart, Prime Minister George Papandreou, will carry out this program, no matter how daunting it may be.'

'I think this is the only way we can restore the stability of the euro," Merkel said. „I'm going to work for the Greece program and its passage.'

Greek Prime Minister George Papandreou promises that he will 'do anything to avoid the country going bankrupt', and announces further spending cuts and tax increases totalling 30 billion euros over three years on top of tough measures already taken. 'These sacrifices will give us breathing space and the time we need to make changes,' Papandreou says, defending the measures.

In a televised cabinet meeting wearing a dark purple tie, the colour used for funerals in Greece Papandreou says, 'It is an unprecedented support package for an unprecedented effort by the Greek people'.

Athen's austerity measures with painful wage and pension cuts are deeply unpopular and trigger widespread protest in Greece with unions planning nationwide strikes.

Jeremy Corbyn Labour MP urges Cameron to write off the Greek debt, 'There is an escalating crisis of Greek society,' he said. 'There is no sane solution to the situation in Greece that involves repaying this debt. The only sensible way forward is to cancel the Greek debt – or at least substantial swaths of it – and for the international community to support Greece's democratically elected government to rebuild its society and its economy. I ask my fellow Labour leadership candidates to echo this call to the prime minister, and for him to heed this call. It is in our own interests to do so.'

November 2010 - Ireland enters bailout programme

The EU and the Irish government agree that the state will be provided €85 billion in EU financial support.

May 2011 - Portugal requests bailout money

Portugal's Prime Minister Mr Socrates announces that his office will be asking for EU financial assistance worth €78bn.

The UK, who doesn't need to be bailed out provides direct funds of €6.5bn (£5 billion) for two bailouts: €3bn for Ireland in November 2010; €3.5bn for Portugal in May 2011.

Sept. 2010 - Ed Miliband becomes Labour leader

As all hope of a coalition with the Liberal Democrats faded in May 2010, Gordon Brown (Lab) resigns with immediate effect. The Deputy Leader, Harriet Harman, steps in as caretaker Leader of the Opposition.

On the same day that Brown stands down, Ed Miliband announces his intention to stand for the leadership position, as do Diane Abbott, Ed Balls, Andy Burnham, and Miliband's older brother David. It's a close race between Ed and his brother but on 25 September 2010 Ed Miliband, aged 40, becomes the youngest-ever leader of the Labour party.

February 2011 - An in-out referendum motion fails

Back in November 2010, Parliament debated a European Union bill, introduced by the Conservative Foreign Secretary William Hague, which would ensure that any amendments to the Lisbon Treaty would be subject to a UK referendum. This stems from the Liberal Democrat Manifesto, now in coalition.

On 1 February 2011 MPs are debating the same bill when Eurosceptic Tory MP Peter Bone tables a motion to trigger a second referendum in the event that the UK public vote 'No' to any treaty change. Mr Bone describes it as a 'binding in-out referendum'.

The House rejects the amendment by 295 votes to 26.
Clearly, Parliament is not willing for an in-out vote just yet.

Now, back to the bill, called The European Union Act 2011 it is passed by the House of Commons on 8 March 2011 by 330 votes to 195 and receives Royal Assent on 19 July 2011.

THE BOTTOM LINE

Any amendment to the Lisbon Treaty will now result in a UK referendum that allows the people to agree to the change, or not.

This demonstrates what little faith the Government has in EU policy makers.

19 July 2011 - A defining day for in-out referendum

The People's Pledge campaign is launched in March 2011 with cross-party support from the start. It is neutral, neither for Remain or Leave. Its only aim is to get a binding in-out referendum on whether Britain should stay in the EU.

They give five main reasons why it's time for an in-out referendum on the EU:

1. Nobody under the age of 54 has ever had the chance to vote on the EU.

2. The EU has now made the majority of laws in the UK.

3. The EU ministers and parliamentarians making those laws were not accountable to British voters.

4. Payments to the EU from the British taxpayer were rising.

5. The European Commission is aiming for more powers of economic governance.

The People's Pledge campaign had support from MPs on both sides of the House: Labour MPs like Kelvin Hopkins, Graham Stringer, and Jon Cruddas; Conservative MPs like Anthony O'Neill; the Mayor of London Boris Johnson; and the Deputy Leader of UKIP David Nuttall. Conservative MP John Baron is the group's chair, and Labour MP and former Government Minister Keith Vaz is vice chair. They get some 128,000 registered voters and 87 MPs to sign up to the campaign by 2012.

From small acorns do oak trees grow

In the initial campaign, voters signed up online and promised to only vote for MPs who support an in-out referendum. The Peoples Pledge says: 'I will only vote at the next election for a candidate who publicly promises to support a binding referendum on our EU membership and to vote for it in the House of Commons.'

The campaign changes tack organizing independent constituency referendums. The first such in Thurrock, Essex, finds that over 80% are in favour of a referendum, with a turnout of 30%. The People's Pledge communications director Ian McKenzie says the poll comes as no surprise.

That result provides enough motivation to organize a postal ballot in two constituencies in Greater Manchester. It is a full postal ballot under the auspices of the Electoral Reform Services to ensure there's no cheating. Campaigning on the ground in the run-up to July are MPs Graham Stringer, a former Leader of Manchester City Council, and David Nuttall. Voting closes on 19 July 2011. Over 85% of voters in both Cheadle and Hazel Grove vote yes to a referendum in the People's Pledge postal ballot, with a turnout of about 35%.

It is their intention to canvas 100 constituencies for a countrywide consensus, but this never happens. They do use YouGov to poll 2,436 voters nationwide and find that 61% would support a referendum, and only 25% would oppose one. The People's Pledge campaign winds up in 2016.

September 2011 - 100,000 sign a referendum petition

A petition with 100,000 signatories is handed in to No.10 calling for an in-out referendum on EU membership.

David Nuttall MEP throws down the gauntlet and prepares a bill to table in Parliament in a few weeks' time. The 100,000 hopefuls who thought their voice counted and could procure change are to have their hopes dashed. Even before the five-hour debate, the result is already decided, as all parties issue a three-line whip to vote the bill down.

The same week as the petition is handed in at No.10, a group of Conservative MPs form the '**European Conservatives and Reformists**' (ECR), whose aim is to discuss steps leading to EU reform as opposed to totally rejecting the EU. The ECR group becomes a Europarty in the European Parliament (to give the UK more influence) and grows as MEPs from other countries join. By 2019 they have 62 MEPs from 15 countries.

October 2011 - Tougher rules on UK immigration

Between 1997-2009, 2.2 million more people settle in Britain than leave. David Cameron wants to cap non-EU migration with tougher controls for those entering from EU counties.

Home Secretary Theresa May is given the task of reforming the rules for illegal immigrants. She says, they must be changed and cites the case of an illegal immigrant who wasn't deported on the grounds that he had to care for his pet cat.

October 2011 - Commons vote on EU referendum

Prompted by the petition signed by more than 100,000 people, David Nuttall tables a motion for a referendum to give people three options: 1) keep the status quo; 2) leave the EU; or 3) reform the terms of the UK's membership of the EU.

The Prime Minister David Cameron says, 'I remain firmly committed to bringing back more powers from Brussels.' going on to say he wanted more reform but now, was not the right time for this three way referendum.

All parties issue a three-line whip, defeating the bill.

The Conservative MP David Davis said, 'We have been told this is the wrong time. This is the time when all the claims of Nicolas Sarkozy and Angela Merkel are to centralise the EU even more to create a fiscal union. It will have an impact on Britain, as the prime minister has said. So this is absolutely the time to think about this. We should be protecting ourselves from the consequences of the eurozone.' Davis continued, 'This was not the invention of some faction of the Conservative party. This was asked for by 100,000 members of the public.'

> **The motion fails by 483 votes to 111**

Although 81 Conservatives and 19 Labour MPs defy the three-line whip voting in favour, this is still not enough to make an impression on the end result.

Nov. 2011 - Eurozone crisis, an opportunity?

Cameron gives a speech calling for fundamental future reform allowing powers to 'ebb back' from Brussels to Westminster. As 81 of his MPs had challenged his authority the previous month voting to support a people's referendum, he goes on to say that leaving the EU is not in Britain's best interest.

Cameron Speaks on Europe at the Lord Mayor's Banquet

'Last year, I spoke about focusing our foreign policy on one objective: promoting Britain's national interest. Tonight I want to explain what that means.'

'In Europe, these are times of change. Old assumptions are collapsing. It was said that no exit from the Euro could ever be envisaged. That membership of the EU would always lead to ever closer union.'

'That rules and structures were like a ratchet - always getting tighter. Powers would only ever go one way. And now everything is changing. Right now, fears about Europe's economic future are understandably intense. Think how the European Union - as it is tonight - looks to those with growing economies watching from Sao Paulo, from Delhi or indeed Washington.'

'Not - as it should be - a place to admire and emulate but a source of alarm and crisis.'

'Britain is not some dispassionate observer. We are a member of the European Union. The strength of our own economy is closely linked to the rest of Europe. So we have a profound national interest in ensuring the swift resolution of the crisis in the Eurozone and a return to growth.'

'What was the European Community, now the EU, has been an effective anchor for democracy and prosperity. But today to the outside world and to the citizens of its own countries the EU's achievements are dramatically overshadowed by its problems. It's not just the crisis in the Eurozone - urgent and all consuming though that is. It's how out of touch the EU has become when its institutions are demanding budget increases while Europe's citizens tighten their belts. It's the pointless interference, rules and regulations that stifle growth not unleash it.'

'The sense that the EU is somehow an abstract end in itself, immune from developments in the real world, rather than a means of helping to deliver better living standards for the people of its Nations. It does not have to be like this. Now is the chance to ask: what kind of Europe do we actually want?'

'For me, the answer is clear. One that is outward-looking with its eyes to the world not gazing inwards. One with the flexibility of a network, not the rigidity of a bloc - whose institutions help by connecting and strengthening its members to thrive in a vibrant world, rather than holding them back.'

'One that understands and values national identity and sees the diversity of Europe's nations as source of strength.'

'So what needs to change? European countries have indulged in debt and overspending and looked uncertain - or worse - when confronted with the consequences. Unless we all get a grip on growth, the European Union will remain an organisation in peril representing a continent in trouble. And now every member of the European Union can see it.'

'For too long, the European Union has tried to make reality fit its institutions. But you can only succeed in the long run if the institutions fit the reality.'

'For years people who have suggested doing less at European level have been accused of not being committed to a successful European Union. But we sceptics have a vital point. We should look sceptically at grand plans and utopian visions. We've a right to ask what the European Union should and shouldn't do, and change it accordingly.'

'As I said, change brings opportunities. An opportunity to begin to refashion the EU so it better serves this nation's interests... and the interests of its other 26 nations too.'

'An opportunity, in Britain's case, for powers to ebb back instead of flow away... and for the European Union to focus on what really matters. To underpin prosperity, stability and growth. That is kind of fundamental reform I yearn for. And I am determined to do everything possible to deliver it.'

Are these the words of a man committed to the EU?

Dec. 2011 - EU Demands tougher monetary controls

Various reasons are cited for the European debt crisis (eurozone crisis). Mainly, that Mediterranean countries and Ireland had been unable to repay their government debt, in other words, they were technically bankrupt. In principle, countries cannot go bankrupt so the money has to be found to prop up their economies until such times when they can work their way out of debt. Assistance came via the European Central Bank (ECB) and the IMF. But the effects of taking on debt are a massive rise in unemployment and low growth.

Austerity is called for, which is so unpopular it causes power shifts as governments are voted out in the hope that the next one will put an end to cut backs. The euro is at risk of being devalued so, at the EU Summit on 9 December 2011, Cameron is asked to join a scheme that will help prop up and stabilize the euro. The UK is asked to pour money into a scheme that could end up devaluing the pound. 'What is on offer isn't in Britain's interests,' says Cameron. He then vetoes the treaty saying: 'It was a tough decision, but the right one.'

The Fiscal Stability Treaty is created and sets out mandatory budget controls for eurozone members.

Cameron gives a statement:

'We want the eurozone countries to come together and solve their problems. But we should only allow that to happen within the EU treaties if there are proper protections for the single market, for other key British interests'.

'Without those safeguards it is better not to have a treaty within a treaty, but have those countries make their arrangements separately.'

The eurozone crisis has meant states who adopted the euro giving up sovereignty in order to stay afloat. Britain needs no such bailout, unlike many EU states.

The European Parliament is displeased with Cameron using his veto and attacks him personally, branding him a coward. Manfred Weber, vice chairman of the European People's Party, is annoyed by Cameron's 'distancing rhetoric' and believes it is ill-advised: 'The country is primarily damaging itself. The British must now decide if they want to be in the EU club or not. ... The game of always wanting to have a say in the debate while also wrecking every compromise is not acceptable in the long run. You can't be a little bit pregnant. ... It must be made clear to Great Britain: Either you want the whole package, or you can leave it alone.' There are calls to put pressure on the UK by taking a clear political stance. Co-chair of the Green group, Daniel Cohn-Bendit, says, 'Now, Cameron is a coward. We must put pressure on the British and force them, by implementing tough regulations on financial markets, to decide if they want out of the EU or if they want to stay inside.'

Cameron replies:

'Britain must now decide its new place in Europe.'
As the EU refuses to meet Cameron's 'safeguards' he decides to veto the Fiscal Stability Treaty. The EU simply bypass Britain

and amend the Lisbon Treaty anyway. France and Germany write up the new accord. The EU are about to gang up 26 to 1 leaving Cameron isolated. Furthermore, the EU plan to punish Britain for not supporting the euro in favour of the pound.

The European Commission President Jose Manuel Barroso expressed that he regretted that unanimity on a treaty change had not been possible: 'Those that have today approved this new fiscal compact have stated that they want to put it as soon as possible into a new fully-fledged treaty, after revision of the current treaties,' he said.

'Having seen it was not possible to get unanimity, it was the proper decision to go ahead at least with those ready to commit immediately. That includes all 17 in the eurozone, plus some who are not in the euro area but want to take part in this fiscal compact.'

**23 countries sign the treaty
without holding a referendum**

When it comes to austerity, people are not wholly enthusiastic. For instance, after a treaty imposing austerity as a condition for receiving bailout funds and continued membership, the people of Greece demonstrate, riot, and burn the EU flag. Reason enough for Greece not to hold a referendum on a treaty creating even more austerity.

The European Union Act 2011 (page 150) calls for a referendum if there are any changes to the Lisbon Treaty. Where was this?

Jan. 2012 - Fiscal Treaty to enforce budget discipline

In an effort to resolve the crisis the **Fiscal Stability Treaty** is drawn up to create a closer fiscal union and to enforce strict budget controls on the 17 eurozone members. This is the treaty Cameron vetoed last December. It is not signed by either the UK or the Czech Republic, as neither use the euro. The Fiscal Stability Treaty clearly gives the EU greater powers by allowing the European Court of Justice to monitor compliance and to impose fines on rule-breakers. It also gives the EC more powers to scrutinize national budgets.

Compared to most other member states, Britain has ridden the money crisis rather well. Cameron's party and the country are behind him; he only has to use the UK's strong position to his advantage and claw back some of the powers given up to Brussels. Statistics show that since the monetary union (single currency) was launched, unemployment in the 17 eurozone states has risen to its highest level, with an average of 10.7% (UK 7.9%). The EC announces that €82 billion (£69 billion) is available to spend on projects to help reduce unemployment across the eurozone and to promote growth.

Douglas Carswell MP (Con) on 31 January 2012 sums up what many MPs are feeling about the Fiscal Stability Treaty:

'From now on it's possible for the rest of the euro club to get together to change the rules and there's now absolutely nothing we can do about it.'

May 2012 - Ireland decides on Fiscal Stability Treaty

On 5 March 2012, 24 European Union leaders sign the European Fiscal Stability Treaty in Brussels. Ireland's Taoiseach (meaning Prime Minister) Mr Enda Kenny signs it, subject to ratification by the electorate in an upcoming referendum.

Ireland, as usual, is bound to hold a referendum, but they employ a trick they used last time. Instead of asking if the people agree with the treaty, or if they want to leave the eurozone, they ask if they can amend the Constitution.

Sinn Féin President Gerry Adams calls for a rejection of the treaty in the referendum, citing that by signing it Ireland will be handing over significant new powers to the European Court of Justice and the European Commission. Adams goes on to say that Mr Kenny is allowing these institutions to impose economic policies on democratically elected governments and to impose heavy fines where they believe these policies have not been adhered to.

The Irish Government is forced to remove some of the content from their website as it promotes a Yes vote in the referendum. It's unconstitutional for a government to spend taxpayers' money to favour one side of a referendum debate.

With 955,091 people voting for and 626,907 against, the treaty was ratified. Ireland, 31 May 2012, vote 60.3% in favour, on a turnout of just 50%

June 2012 - EU renegotiation becomes necessary

More than 90 Conservative MPs sign a letter from John Baron asking for legislation committing the UK to an EU referendum after the next election. The letter says the law would 'address the lack of public trust' as past promises to hold such a vote never materialized.

David Cameron makes a clear statement to the House of Commons: 'There are those who argue for an in-out referendum now. I don't agree with that because I don't believe leaving the EU would be best for Britain.'

'I completely understand why some people want an in-out referendum. Some people just want to get out: stop the bus, I want to get off. But I don't share that view. That is not the right thing to do. The problem with an in-out referendum is that it only gives people those two choices. You can stay either in with all the status quo or you can get out. Most people in Britain want a government that stands up and fights within Europe and gets the things we want in Europe; that changes some of the relationships we have in Europe. I have made some small steps forward.'

Conservative Foreign Secretary William Hague says that he believes most people want a better relationship with Europe and that leaving would have too many disadvantages. He goes on to admit that there are disadvantages to being in the EU and the time to decide about our relationship with Europe is when we know whether we can get that better relationship.

Liam Fox MP (Con) says that unless there is a rebalancing of relationships within the EU, Britain should leave.

July 2012 - Barroso lashes out at UK MEPs

President of the European Commission José Manuel Barroso tells the European Parliament that he is puzzled by the behaviour of British Conservative MEPs of the ECR group, as they seem to take delight in the difficulties of the eurozone. He's referring to Conservative MEP Martin Callanan, who had repeatedly criticized bank bailouts as wasting taxpayers' money and talked in favour of eurozone exits for some states.

Barroso went on to say that this is not just a eurozone problem but a European one. The British Government has given more money to its banks than any other European state. Since 2008 the UK has committed €82.9 billion to UK banks and a further €40.41 billion in interventions and guarantees - amounting to €158 billion.

Total UK taxpayers' money propping up the financial sector is €281.31 billion.

Cameron talks about the public being given the opportunity for 'fresh consent', meaning a general election, but he is still not backing any sort of referendum. Back in the House of Commons, MPs keep up the pressure for a referendum.

Sept. 2012 - Barroso's State of the Union speech

EC President José Manuel Barroso gives his State of the Union speech on 12 September 2012. He says; 'Europe needs a new direction, new thinking. Globalization demands more European unity, more European unity demands more integration, more integration demands more democracy, **European democracy**.' He recognizes that the EU needs to reform and calls for a debate on major reforms to make the European Union a 'federation of nation states'.

Nigel Farage gives a statement on Barroso's State of the Union address. He criticizes Mario Draghi for the bailouts to keep Mediterranean countries tied to the EU, countries that should never have been allowed to join (since they never fulfilled the criteria).

He concludes by saying:

'And I think Mr. Barroso, today, the British people hearing you calling for the EU to become a global power, making it absolutely clear that members states must obey, must obey what you tell them whether they are in the relatively wealthy north or the poorer south. I think those comments - this emerging, creeping, euro dictatorship - is something that will repulse millions of British people and the only good news I take from today is, you've helped to bring that referendum just a little bit closer.'

Oct. 2012 - European Communities Act 1972 (Repeal)

Conservative MP Douglas Carswell attempts to repeal the European Communities Act 1972, which would take the UK out of the EU and revert to being a member of the former European Economic Community. Carswell admits the bill has little chance of becoming law but feels the option should at least be debated in the House. As expected, it gets nowhere.

On its second reading, Douglas Carswell talks to a near-empty House of Commons - demonstrating MP's disrespect for the electorate. This is the first crowdsourced legislation, Carswell explains that more than 5,000 readers of his website decided what Private Member's bill he should propose.

Seven years later this very Act is repealed

On 18 August 2019 the Secretary of State for Exiting the EU, Steve Barclay, signs the commencement order which will repeal the European Communities Act 1972 on exit day, bringing the European Withdrawal Act MPs voted through in September 2018 into force.

> *Cameron has been tested to the limit this year as constant pressure to hold a referendum makes him feel pushed into a corner. The euro crisis is a wakeup call for many Tory rebels as Cameron's veto to protect the pound left him isolated.*

October 2012 - Government loses EU budget vote

An embarrassing defeat for the coalition Government as MPs demand reductions in the EU budget. They turn down the proposed EU budget for 2014-2020 by 307 votes to 294.

Mark Reckless MP (Con) says 'voters will find it hard to understand why there are cuts to UK public spending but that the EU is getting a larger budget.' He goes on to say that we simply cannot afford an increase from €9.2 billion in one year to €13.6 billion the next.

Leaving aside the row about the EU budget, The Daily Telegraph reports William Hague's speech:

'If we cannot show that decision-making can flow back to national parliaments then the system will become democratically unsustainable. ... Public disillusionment with the EU in Britain is the deepest it has ever been.'

There is talk about including a proposal in the next Conservative manifesto for the repatriation of powers from the EU back to Westminster. The Fresh Start Group - a moderate Eurosceptic pressure group formed back in September 2011 by three Conservative MPs - is certainly looking into it. Any negotiation on reforms to allow powers to 'ebb back' from Brussels to Westminster (as cited in Cameron's speech of November 2011) will require tough negotiators.

Scottish independence referendum deal signed

The Scots were yearning for home rule long before the year 1306, when Robert the Bruce was made King of the House of Stuart. Anyway, Cameron signs a deal on 15 October 2012 to allow a single-question referendum on Scottish independence to be held before the end of 2014.

November 2012 - Farage on Merkel's UK visit

Angela Merkel meets David Cameron in London to discuss the EU budget for 2014-2020, just prior to the forthcoming summit. Farage talks about growing EU hostility toward the United Kingdom's membership and blame against anglo-saxon markets in London and New York for the faults of the eurozone, asking Chancellor Merkel to pass this message on to Mr. Cameron: 'This simply doesn't work any more, it really is time that the United Kingdom left the EU. He hasn't got the courage to say it himself, but, if you say it to him, it may have an impact. All I'm suggesting Chancellor, is that we have a simple amicable divorce, and then we'll all get on much better in the future.'

Farage just before the summit says: 'Mr Cameron heads to Brussels tomorrow, I think on "mission impossible". But it is a remarkable debate to think that the European Union is talking about taking another trillion euros from European taxpayers despite the fact that the accounts have not been signed off for 18 years in a row. If this was a company, the directors, or in this case the Commission, would all be in prison.'

Nov. 2012 - EU summit ends without agreement

Cameron goes to the Brussels summit to negotiate the UK's contribution to the EU budget. In view of the defeat in the House of Commons last October he'll request a freeze - only paying the same amount as the previous year. In the end, Britain and Germany refuse to sign off the €971 billion budget for 2014-2020. The President of the European Council, Herman Van Rompuy, calls it a day, with no deal. They have three months to agree an acceptable offer.

Cameron says: "I believe it would be wrong for the European budget to increase at a time when we are having to make difficult decisions not just in Britain but all over the European Union to get our budgets back to balancing. That's why I've said it should be at best a cut, at worst a freeze.'

December 2012 - EU receives the Nobel peace prize

The armaments manufacturer Alfred Nobel invented TNT. He was so upset by how the military used his invention that he created a foundation to award an annual prize to someone who promoted peace.

The EU wins it for building a 'continent of peace', the first time an institution is awarded a Nobel. It is presented to the heads of the EU's three main institutions: Herman Van Rompuy, President of the European Council; Jose Manuel Barroso, President of the European Commission; and Martin Schulz, President of the European Parliament.

December 2012 - Predictions wrong about eurozone

London Mayor Boris Johnson gives a speech explaining that when the UK decided not to join the eurozone (the name given to those who adopted the euro) many large institutions, such as the Confederation of British Industry, and economic thinkers said that London's financial markets would never survive outside the eurozone; that business would all go to Frankfurt. Against all these negative predictions London remains one of the largest financial centres in the world, with 40% of trade being done in euros, and it exports financial services to the tune of £17 billion each year. The dire warnings of doom and gloom were unfounded, while Eurosceptic predictions turned out to be entirely correct. The euro is a ,calamitous project'.

The EU took a battering in the eurozone crisis and a new world is emerging. Payments from richer states to the EU are bound to increase as the poorer EU member States still need propping up. There has been unrest in those countries where austerity is hardest, Athens, Paris, and Madrid all experience violent protests.

Cameron dodges and weaves all year, under constant pressure from the Eurosceptics in his own party, voters handing in petitions, and popularity gains by UKIP, led by Nigel Farage who is given lots of air time.

Does the Conservative Party blame David Cameron for not clinching an absolute majority in the last election? Do they see the coalition with the Liberal Democrats as a humiliation?

A flurry of radical Conservative backbenchers have been waging a lively debate for months promoting a referendum.

Cameron refuses to even consider a referendum in 2012. He resists it at every turn and only talks about Britain negotiating a new relationship. He is right to question the EC's growing EU budget, and the lack of democracy in the EU executive and EU decision-making.

It's not clear what laws and regulations Cameron wants to claw back from the EU. The German Chancellor, the French President, and all the other European leaders lose patience with him. It seems that Britain wants to pick and choose policies via a long list of opt-outs, while everyone else must accept the lot. Cameron thinks Britain should remain in the EU and negotiate a better relationship, but he doesn't say what Britain expects of Europe.

With the next general election two and a half years away, in May 2015, much can happen.

PMQs on 16 January 2013 - The Opposition Leader Edward Miliband crosses swords with Cameron on his long-awaited statement on 'Britain and Europe'.

Ed Miliband: 'When the prime minister first became leader of the Conservative party, he said that its biggest problem was that it spent far too much of its time "banging on" about Europe. Is he glad those days are over?'
'What is the prime minister's answer, to the question: will Britain be in the European Union in five years' time?'

David Cameron: 'My view is that Britain is better off in the European Union, but it is right for us to see the changes taking place in Europe, and to ensure that we argue for the changes that Britain needs, so that we have a better relationship between Britain and Europe, a better organised European Union, and the full-hearted consent of the British people. Those are the choices that we are making.'

Miliband: 'Maybe we are making a bit of progress. In October 2011, as I am sure the prime minister will remember, he and I walked shoulder to shoulder through the Lobby against the 81 Conservative members who voted for an in-out referendum. You might call it two parties working together in the national interest. At the time, the Foreign Secretary - I think he was on his way to Australia to get as far away from the prime minister's speech as possible - said that the reason for our vote was that an in-out referendum. Was the Foreign Secretary right?'

The prime minister: 'I do not think it would be right for Britain to have an in-out referendum today, because we would be giving the British people a false choice. Millions of people in this country, myself included, want Britain to stay in the European Union, but they believe that there are chances to negotiate a better relationship.'

See what happens just seven days later...

CHAPTER SEVEN

SEVEN YEARS
OF HELL

January 2013 - The speech that changes everything

Prime Minister David Cameron gives an earth-shattering speech on Britain and Europe on 23 January 2013 at 8:45 am. It's a defining moment as he calls for an in-out referendum.

Don't get me wrong, it's a defining moment not because it causes Brexit but, for 38 years the British people have been denied a say in their own destiny, which he now rectifies.

His Britain and Europe speech lasts about 38 minutes. Cameron says he wants to negotiate the UK's relationship with the EU and then give people the 'simple choice' between staying in under those new terms or leave the EU.

PMQs are a heated debate, now the cat is out of the bag.

For the first time an in-out referendum's on the table

PMQs, Bill Cash tables a question: 'My right honourable friend insists on five excellent principles, including democracy based on national parliaments, and he rejects ever closer union. Other member states want to go ahead with more integration and are demanding it.'

'Last year on the Fiscal Stability Treaty they ignored his veto and went ahead irrespective of the rules of the European Union. Will my right honourable friend [Cameron] tell us what will happen if by next spring they insist on going ahead with their own intended proposals and what will he do in response?'

Cameron replies: 'I believe what is going to happen, is that the eurozone countries do need to make changes to the European Union, they are changing the union to fix the currency. That is what the four Presidents' report is about, and it poses quite wide ranging treaty changes.'

'I think this frankly gives us the right to argue that for those countries that are not in the eurozone, and frankly I believe are never going to join the eurozone, that there are changes that we would like, not just for ourselves but for a more open, competitive and flexible Europe.'

'So, there is going to be change in Europe, the eurozone countries do need to make changes but we should not back off from pushing forward our agenda as well.'

February 2013 - UK contributions to the EU Budget

A proposed cut of €34.4 billion (£29 billion) over the next seven years is agreed. UK Contributions to the EU budget will go up, but not by as much as first thought.

May 2013 - Draft EU referendum bill is drawn up

A draft bill is published by David Cameron that outlines Conservative plans for renegotiation and promises an in-out vote if they're returned to office in 2015.

John Baron MP (Con) tables a separate bill on 16 May 2013 to guarantee a referendum by 2017. It is defeated by 277 votes to 130 as 114 Conservative MPs ignore a three-line whip voting it down. The bill is doomed even before the debates have started.

July 2013 - EU referendum bill passes 2nd reading

Just two months later, the draft bill drawn up by David Cameron is introduced by James Wharton MP (Con). It requires the holding of a referendum on the UK's continued membership of the EU before the end of 2017. The question as set out in the bill is: 'Do you think that the United Kingdom should be a member of the European Union?'

On its second reading 5 July 2013 it passes by 304 votes to nil. Almost all Labour MPs and all Liberal Democrat MPs abstain.

Nov. 2013 - Referendum bill gets House approval

The EU referendum bill tabled by Conservative MP James Wharton passes its final stage in the Commons, despite the efforts of Labour and Liberal Democrat MPs to sabotage it.

The bill is given a third reading on 29 November 2013 and sent to the House of Lords for consideration in January next year. The bill gets a second reading January 2014 in the House of Lords but does not become law. It is essentially blocked by the House of Lords, who describe it as 'economically devastating' and 'biased and vague'.

Speaking outside the chamber, Mr Wharton MP says: 'Labour and the Lib-Dems conspired in the House of Lords to kill this important piece of legislation, doing the bidding of their political masters in the Commons.'

Mike Gapes, a Labour MP comments: 'This bill is a disgrace. It should not be supported. I hope the House of Lords will do justice to it and amend it significantly'.

With the bill now dead in the water, Prime Minister David Cameron says: 'As Labour and the Lib-Dems have killed the Wharton bill, the one way to guarantee a referendum is to vote Conservative at the next General Election.'

David Cameron says the Conservatives will bring back the bill and use the Parliament Act to force it into law, rather than see the Lords block it again.

March 2014 - Nick Clegg and Nigel Farage TV debate

In the run-up to the European Parliamentary elections, Deputy Prime Minister Nick Clegg and UKIP leader Nigel Farage go head to head in two TV debates to make sense of the biggest question the UK faces this century.

Two sides of the coin are very well presented during two hours of debate as Clegg claims to be the party for Remain and Farage the face of the Leave movement.

Leader of the Opposition, Ed Miliband announces in an article in the Financial Times that he'll take on the same policy as the Conservatives, saying that Labour ,strongly believes Britain's future is in the EU', adding:

'We will do the right thing for our national interest…and send out a message that under Labour, Britain is open for business.' - But he acknowledges the need for EU reform:

'The British people know that the history of the EU, as well as uncertainty about precisely what a changing Europe and an integrating eurozone might involve, means that a further transfer of powers remains possible.'

'So, I am announcing that the next Labour government will legislate for a new lock: there would be no transfer of powers from the UK without a referendum on our continued membership of the EU.'

May 2014 - European Parliament elections

The European Parliament (EP) elections on 22 May 2014 coincide with local elections in England and Northern Ireland.

There are 73 seats up for grabs for the lucky MEPs who can persuade the public to actually get out and vote. The turnout is only 35.6%, even after the four main parties have spent nearly £8.5 million on campaigning.

It seems to me, there is more engagement in the Eurovision Song Contest than in who will represent Britain's interests in Europe. The 2014 European elections cost the UK taxpayer £109 million. This money pays for polling stations and venues, mailing out candidate information and polling cards, transport to facilitate counting of votes, and so on.

UKIP promoting their Leave campaign are without doubt, the big winners in 2014. They gain 11 seats taking 24 seats in total and get 27% of the popular vote. Labour win 20 seats and the Conservatives 19. The Liberal Democrats, who spent £1.5 million on campaigning, win just one seat.

Where are the Remain voters in this election?

This is a defining moment when the whole Brexit debacle could be put to rest once and for all. A meagre 35.6% of voters bother to turn out, of which 27% vote for UKIP. This gives Nigel Farage the platform to push his agenda.
A missed opportunity to stop Brexit,
... Strike One!

The European Parliament has its own 'parties'

After the UK elect their 73 MEPs, the wrangling begins as 751 MEPs align themselves with a Europarty that has shared political interests and build alliances within the European Parliament. The party with the most MEPs has most power in Parliament and for a majority, a party needs 376 seats/MEPs.

The two largest parties are the European People's Party (EPP), with 221 seats, and the Progressive Alliance of Socialists and Democrats (S&D), with 191 seats.

There are eight such Europarties, including smaller ones like Europe of Freedom and Direct Democracy (EFDD) with 48 seats, which UKIP aligns with, and the European Conservatives and Reformists (ECR) with 70 seats, who can definitely count on the Conservatives as they formed this Europarty back in September 2011 to break away from the EPP.

As the newly elected MEPs gather in the EU Parliament on 25 May 2014 and begin to pledge allegiance to a particular party, a TV screen shows which party is getting the most MEPs in real time.

No single Europarty gets a majority, so a grand coalition is formed between the EPP and the S&D.

Next on the agenda for the newly elected MEPs is to decide on who will become EC President.

How did Jean-Claude Juncker become EC President?

When the mandate of Commission President José Manuel Barroso expires in November 2014 (he has held the seat for ten years), a new President needs to be found.

The President of the EC is the most senior executive official of the EU who leads the Commission in its work of proposing and enforcing EU legislation, implementing policies, and managing the EU budget. It's therefore really important to have someone trustworthy.

New rules laid out in the Lisbon Treaty changed how the next Commission President is to be chosen. Article 17 of the Lisbon Treaty gives Parliament the right to elect the Commission President: 'Taking into account the elections of the European Parliament and after having held the appropriate consultations, the European Council through qualified majority shall propose to the European Parliament a candidate for the next president of the Commission. This one candidate shall be elected by the European Parliament by a majority of its members.'

As MEPs begin to align themselves with Europarties, those running for President of the EC are already jockeying for position. There are no presidential candidates from the UK.

Mr Hannes Swoboda, President of the S&D, says to delegates attending the EP that, any Commission President must be one for change and not for more of the same.

The presidential Line-up from the five main parties

➤ European People's Party (EPP) - Mr Jean-Claude Juncker, a politician since 1984, with many years in high office and Prime Minister of Luxembourg 1995-2013.

➤ Socialists and Democrats (S&D) - Mr Martin Schulz (Germany), had served on his local council and as Mayor; elected as MEP in 1994; President of the European Parliament 2012-2017.

➤ Liberals (ALDE) - Mr Guy Verhofstadt (Belgium), elected as MEP in 2009; made President of the group.

➤ Greens - Ms Ska Keller (Germany), by far the youngest candidate in the race (33-years-old); born in 1981 she is a member of the Green Party Germany and co-President of the Greens/EFA groups in the EP.

➤ European Left - Mr Alexis Tsipras (Greece), stood as MEP in 2014 for the first time; the youngest-ever Prime Minister of Greece from 2015-2019, he negotiated the Greek bailouts.

Even though the general public get no say in who gets the job, a live debate between the five candidates is televised across 30 countries in May 2014.

The most vocal and public adversary to Juncker is definitely David Cameron. Angela Merkel is also against Juncker, but even more against Schulz. And the other three candidates? Well ... ? The candidates offered by the Lib-Dems and the Green party lack experience (great to have on board but not to run the show), and as for Alexis Tsipras becoming the most powerful person in Europe? I shudder to think. So, there are only two big guns in the running (Schulz vs Juncker), making it a two-horse race.

Back in March 2014, Angela Merkel attends an EPP congress in Dublin where it's to be decided who their candidate for Commission President will be. Merkel supports Juncker's nomination against his opponent Michel Barnier of France. Her motivation is to stop Schulz, and only Juncker can achieve this. She goes further than just backing Juncker, she lobbies other leaders to support the Luxembourger, believing that Juncker has a far better chance of winning in Brussels than Schulz.

Meanwhile, Cameron is ramping up his 'Stop Juncker' campaign. He says publicly on the 17 June that he will 'fight right to the end' against the principle of giving the most powerful job in the EU to the candidate of the strongest party in European Parliament elections (the EPP in this case). Given the QMV principle, Cameron needs allies, which he thinks he has in the Dutch and Swedish Prime Ministers. He is wrong.

The only name on the list who looks increasingly likely to be nominated at the leader's summit in June is Juncker.

EC has first choice

Although Jean-Claude Juncker is disliked by Sweden, the Netherlands, and Italy he manages to win their support. For the first time, the nomination of Commission President is put to the European Council for a formal vote: 26 member states vote for Jean-Claude Juncker (EPP); two - UK PM David Cameron and Hungarian PM Viktor Orbán - vote against him.

Cameron made it clear that he wants to block the system. As he arrives at the Harpsund meeting Cameron calls for „less pointless interference" in the EU, adding: 'The democratically elected leaders of the EU should be the ones who choose who should run these institutions rather than accept some new process which was never agreed.' Cameron continues;

'Juncker did not candidate anywhere and was not elected by anyone," Cameron wrote. „The citizens who went to the polls wanted to vote for their MEPs, not the President of the Commission. The future of the European Union is at stake. Either it is reforming, or it's going downhill.'

Did Cameron's actions and the 'Stop Juncker' campaign ruin any chance to negotiate better terms for Britain in the future?

On 2 July 2014, during an EP debate, Farage forecasts that the UK will leave the EU and says to Philippe Lamberts, MEP of the Greens group, 'Don't worry too much about my presence, because in the next five years I won't be here.'

On 10 July 2014, just before the parliamentary vote, the EFDD group chaired by Nigel Farage puts questions to Jean-Claude Juncker, who will become the most powerful man in Europe if he gets a majority of the votes in the EP the following week.

> Only one candidate is put forward for the position of President of the EC, on 15 July 2014. The European Parliament elects Jean-Claude Juncker, 422 votes to 307.

November 2014 - Massive tax-avoidance

The real arguments about Juncker's suitability only take place after he gets the job. A review of leaked confidential documents shows that during Juncker's time as Prime Minister of Luxembourg, companies channelled hundreds of billions of dollars through Luxembourg, saving billions in taxes.

Guy Verhofstadt, Leader of the S&Ds, requests that Juncker come to the European Parliament next week to explain the urgent action they intend to take to fight tax evasion and tax fraud. Juncker cancels his participation at the last moment.

However, Juncker's party, the EPP group considers this is 'a personal issue' for Commission President Juncker and expresses trust that, under his leadership, the EU executive will step up efforts to combat tax evasion and tax fraud.

December 2014 - Nigel Farage welcomes Juncker

Farage welcomes 'Team Juncker' with his famous words: 'Mr Juncker, you are competent, dangerous and doomed to fail.'

Farage then predicts that Juncker will spend most of his time during the next five years dealing with the Greek debt crisis and with Britain wanting to leave the EU.

Annual cost of the European Parliament per inhabitant:

Germany	€9.20 per inhabitant/year
United Kingdom	€8.90 per inhabitant/year
France	€8.00 per inhabitant/year
USA	€6.00 per inhabitant/year

All member states contribute, plus America. Do the American people know that they are paying for a parliament in which they have no say? How did the EU wangle that one?

September 2014 - Scottish Independence Vote

With 84.6% of the Scottish population getting out to vote in the Scottish independence referendum, 55.3% (2,001,926) vote against independence. The 1,617,989 voters who want to leave will be heard for many years to come. Scotland has been part of the United Kingdom since 1707. The Scottish referendum cost the British taxpayer £15,850,000.

October 2014 - The Conservative Party Conference

A very moving speech from David Cameron on 1 October 2014 lays out Tory future plans. He announces a package worth £7 billion in tax cuts by 2020. He warns that a vote for UKIP will let Labour back into power. At the 43-minute mark he talks about migration from within the EU and promises to renegotiate terms with the EU. Excerpts from that speech:

'But we know the bigger issue today is migration from within the EU, immediate access to our welfare system, paying benefits to families back at home, employment agencies signing up people from overseas not recruiting here. Numbers that have increased faster than we in this country wanted and at a level that was too much for our communities and for our labour markets. All of this has to change, and it will be at the very heart of my renegotiation strategy to Europe.'

'Britain, I know you want this sorted so I will go to Brussels, I will not take no for an answer, and when it comes to free movement, I will get what Britain needs and anyone who thinks I can't or won't deliver this I would say judge me by my record. I'm the first prime minister to veto a treaty, the first prime minister to cut the European budget, and yes, I pulled us out of those European bailout schemes as well. Around that table in Europe they know I say what I mean, and I mean what I say.'

'So, we're going to go in as a country, we're going to get our powers back, we're going to fight for our national interest and yes, we will put it to a referendum, in or out it will be your choice, and let the message go out from this hall: it is only with the Conservatives that you will get that choice.'

'Of course, it's not just the European Union that needs sorting out – it's the European Court of Human Rights. When that charter was written, in the aftermath of the Second World War, it set out the basic rights we should respect. But since then, interpretations of that charter have led to a whole lot of things that are frankly wrong. Rulings to stop us deporting suspected terrorists. The suggestion that you've got to apply the human rights convention even on the battle-fields of Helmand. And now – they want to give prisoners the vote. I'm sorry, I just don't agree. Our Parliament – the British Parliament – decided they shouldn't have that right. This is the country that wrote Magna Carta, the country that time and again has stood up for human rights, whether liberating Europe from fascism or leading the charge today against sexual violence in war.'

'Let me put this very clearly: We do not require instruction on this from judges in Strasbourg. So at long last, with a Conservative Government after the next election, this country will have a new British Bill of Rights to be passed in our Parliament and as for Labour's Human Rights Act? We will scrap it, once and for all.

'So that's what we offer: a Britain that everyone is proud to call home.'

A rousing speech, but then this happens....

October 2014 - The Surprise invoice for £1.7 billion

Once upon a time in a distant land, far, far away,
the emperor of Airy Fairy town had binged the funds away.
Grizzle, fizzle, bubble, and sizzle who will pay the bills?
Don't despair, I know a place the kingdom over yonder hill.
Sir Dodgy Dave's got loads o' dosh and even money to burn.
A facts a fact, they've got the cash, it's more than we can earn.
So, legislation comes to pass, and all the bets are on,
If Cameron's going to knuckle down and simply pay thereon.

It would be funny, if it wasn't true.

Out of the blue, the EU sends an invoice to the UK Treasury on Friday 17 October 2014 for a 'top-up' contribution to the value of €2.1 billion (£1.7 billion), demanding payment by Monday 1 December 2014.

This surprise extra EU budget contribution is apparently for recalculated underpayments over the past four years. Contributions are calculated on the basis of gross national income. Britain's economy had done better than expected, the eurozone's worse, so some countries get a bill, others receive a rebate. As you will see most are getting money back.

In addition to the recalculated budget contributions, they also demand that the UK pay Germany and France €780 million and €1.16 billion respectively in refunds.

The UK is not alone. After receiving a surprise bill for €642 million a senior Dutch official says, 'We were very surprised and have lots of questions'.

Judging by the following graph the UK economy must have been running on steroids. The graph only shows those countries who paid extra or got money back (in euro billions).

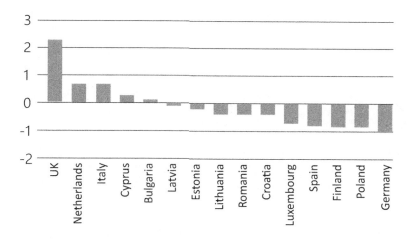

Leaders get wind of these bills while attending an EU summit in Brussels. David Cameron says that 'it is an unacceptable way for this organization (EU) to work - to suddenly present a bill like this for such a vast sum of money, with so little time to pay it. And it is an unacceptable way to treat one of the biggest contributors to the European Union. ... it has never been the case that a two billion euro bill has suddenly been presented. It is not acceptable, and it is an appalling way to behave and I am not paying the bill.'

The UK tries to negotiate a reduction of the surcharge with European finance ministers arguing that 'the sum cannot be challenged.' Cameron gives a speech to the House of Commons rejecting the surcharge and refusing to pay it.

Was this punishment for Cameron's 'Stop Junker' campaign?

Treasury aides to the Chancellor of the Exchequer, George Osborne, concede that Britain will pay £850 million while not cashing a €1 billion rebate cheque. The bill is paid to the EU in full. The Conservatives claim they've halved the bill, stating that they'd only actually be paying £850 million. All that spin!

26 October 2014 - EU referendum bill tabled again

Conservative backbencher Bob Neill MP again tables a private member's bill for an EU referendum. Before a referendum can take place, it requires legislation from Parliament.

October 2014 - Tories accuse Lib-Dems of blocking

Mr Bob Neill accuses coalition partner, the Lib-Dems, of using tricks to block the bill, which fails to progress further.

The duly elected Parliament are still blocking the way, 22 months after Cameron had promised an in-out referendum.

> **This is now the sixth time in as many years that an in-out referendum bill has been rejected by Parliament.**

November 2014 - Levelling the playing field

The UK immigration system is dysfunctional and in absolute chaos. With over 2,500 potential migrants in Calais desperately trying to cross the channel, and some 50,000 rejected asylum seekers recently gone AWOL, the Home Office are obviously not coping. Health tourism is a big issue in the press. The government's failure to implement proper IT systems tracking asylum seekers has made the situation even worse. Cases are mounting up, some going as far back as 2007. Caseworkers dealing with a dysfunctional system are not motivated and morale is low due to the heavy workload, day after day.

The UK's public conception is that, there are millions of migrants and millions of European immigrants milking Britain's benefit system. But the real headache for most people is freedom of movement of labour from Eastern Bloc countries within the EU, which has been going on since 2003.

Why do British people think like this?

The statistics show

In 2013, 21,275 children were born to Polish women in the UK.

In 2014 the largest ethnic group in the UK (after Indians) is 790,000 Polish nationals - 1% of the population and more than Irish-born residents. This figure rises to 911,000 by 2016.

The Poles are escaping an economy in a mess and a country rated the 36th most corrupt in the world (World Economic

Forum - WEF). But how do you build up the economy of your country when so many people move out? (56 million live outside, 38 million live in Poland) The people with the gumption to get off their asses and do something have all left.

In 2003 the Czech Republic, Hungary, and Poland didn't meet the criteria for joining the EU but were admitted anyway. Even after the EU invests €862 billion of taxpayers' money into these countries, they still fail to meet the criteria for joining.

On the WEF corruption scale the Czech Republic ranks 38th, Hungary ranks 64th. What has happened to the €862 billion?

So, is migration a benefit to developed countries like the UK? During the 1960s boom period it made sense to encourage migrants. Germany, for example sent teams to Yugoslavia to bring back workers, paying for their transport and accommodation. Most migrants send around 20% of their pay packet back to their home country, where it has a higher value due to differences in the cost of living. During a recession, the wages of low-skilled workers get suppressed. This puts the most vulnerable people at most risk. They pay little in UK taxes due to low wages and add little to the UK economy because of sending any spare money home. Let's look to the future. Most will probably return to their place of origin for their retirement, being able to live extremely well on a British pension. Again, not spending that money in the UK. I am a migrant myself. I moved to Germany more than 20 years ago and although I have never sent money home, it has given me the opportunity to earn a good wage. Most of the

Brits I know here will probably retire to the UK on a German pension, which is at least 25% higher than a UK pension. But I digress.

Germany has a policy that nobody can claim benefits from the state unless they have paid into the system. If you arrive and don't work then you are considered a tourist. Everyone who lives in Germany must register with a local office so the government knows exactly where every single resident is at any one time and it's law that everyone must carry an ID card.

It has taken the UK government eleven years to come up with the same policy for the UK to operate on a level playing field with other developed states in the EU. Except that in the UK, the press describe it as:

Cameron announces tough new measures

Cameron announces measures to bring the UK in line with other EU nations like Germany. Not so exciting as how the UK press present it as 'tough new measures', in view of public sentiment of the day. The new measures are:

➤ EU migrants can no longer claim child benefit for dependents living outside the UK.

(2018, Germany sets up an investigation unit when they discover that 50% of all family allowances go abroad.)

➤ EU migrants must wait four years before claiming in-work benefits, such as tax credits, or getting a council house.

> If someone arriving from the EU has not found work within six months, then they have to leave the UK.

> Restricting the right of EU migrants who want to bring non-EU family members into the UK.

> Universal Credit is not available to EU jobseekers.

> Quicker deportation of convicted criminals.

> Longer re-entry bans for beggars and fraudsters removed from the UK.

> Migrants from 'new' member states will not be allowed UK entry until their economies have 'converged more closely'.

> Extra money for communities with high levels of migrants.

None of the nine points mentioned here are ever tabled for negotiation with the EU. A year later Cameron comes up with a watered-down four-point version not coming close to what is proposed here.

There are more people from Poland living in the UK than from any other Eastern Bloc nation. When 2.6% of your population has moved to the UK and there is a risk of them not receiving child benefits or not being able to send 20% or their earnings back home, the Polish Government must act.

Mr Rostowski is an MP in Warsaw, Poland, and 800,000 of his constituents live in the UK, they have representation.

Mr Rostowski sees Cameron's speech as discriminatory

and threatens that his Government will use its power to veto any plan in the EU. Cameron's proposals would change the Lisbon Treaty and will require an amendment and therefore backing from Brussels to put it in place. Cameron is to present his demands to the President of the European Council, Mr Donald Tusk (who is himself from Poland).

May 2015 - Conservatives win with a majority

By winning a 12 seat majority, Cameron can lose the shackles of a coalition with the Lib-Dems that have stopped him pursuing an in-out referendum. The in-out referendum was a key issue in Cameron's election campaign. Here was yet another missed opportunity to avoid Brexit.
... Strike Two!

The biggest winners though are the SNP, who now have 56 seats, commanding practically the whole of Scotland. The Lib-Dems go from 57 seats to just eight and, as Cameron says, 'they can now hold their party conference in a taxi'.

Labour's Ed Miliband and the Lib-Dems' Nick Clegg resign as party leaders. Farage's resignation is refused by his party and he remains as leader.

8. May, Cameron stands outside No.10 to give the traditional speech immediately after visiting Buckingham Palace, 'Together, we can make Great Britain greater still.' He acts quickly on his promise to call a referendum should the Conservatives are returned to power.

May 2015 - Queen's Speech includes EU referendum

Parliamentarians are invited to hear the Queen's Speech which lays out her Government's agenda, on 27 May 2015. She says;

'Legislation will be introduced to provide for an in-out referendum on membership of the European Union before the end of 2017'

➢ On 28 May 2015, the day after the Queen's Speech, Foreign Secretary Philip Hammond introduces the European Union Referendum Act 2015 to the House.

➢ On 9 June 2015, at its second reading, MPs vote 544 to 53 in favour of the principle of holding a referendum.

➢ On its third reading on 7 September 2015, MPs vote 316 to 53 in favour (281 abstain), the bill becomes law and receives Royal Assent on 15 December 2015.

This is the seventh occasion that an in-out referendum bill is presented to the House of Commons and this time it passes with such ease.

It just goes to show the power of the Queen's Speech!

The Lords and MPs might show little respect for the British public who voted them in but, they would never disrespect the Queen.

June 2015 - Cameron speaks to the EC

This is a defining moment, as Cameron explains to the heads of state the seriousness of recent events. Here are three excerpts from his speech to the European Commission.

'I had three clear objectives for this summit: to ensure that there's a comprehensive approach to the migration crisis; to push for faster progress on the Digital Single Market; but most importantly, to get the UK renegotiation underway ...'

'... on renegotiating the UK's relationship with the European Union. The European Union needs to change. Britain's relationship with the European Union needs to change, and I've got a plan to achieve that: reform, renegotiation and referendum. Now we're already making progress on reforming the EU. We've cut the EU budget, we've cut the EU red tape, we're getting on with completing the single market, but this is not enough. We need more substantive reform in four particular areas: sovereignty, fairness, competitiveness and immigration ...'

'... people in Britain rightly think that the EU interferes too much, that too many decisions are taken too far away from them, and that they absolutely are clear about one thing. They and I do not want to be part of an ever-closer union to be dragged into a state called Europe. That may be for others, but it will never be for Britain, and it is time to recognize that specifically.'

Sept. 2015 - With 59.5% Corbyn is Labour Leader

Following the resignation of Ed Miliband there are only two contenders and Jeremy Corbyn is elected Leader of the Labour Party on 12 September 2015. Only four days later he is standing opposite David Cameron in the House at PMQs.

October 2015 - The campaign groups are launched

Groups are created to represent each side of the argument in the forthcoming 2016 in-out referendum.

Two political strategists start a group to promote leaving the EU, which the Electoral Commission designate as the official organization in favour of leaving the European Union.

Created by Matthew Elliott and Dominic Cummings they bring together MPs from both sides of the House, including such big guns in British politics as Michael Gove, Boris Johnson, Iain Duncan Smith, Liam Fox, and Lord Owen.

A newly formed company, The In Campaign Ltd., is launched and creates the 'Stronger In' campaign. They also have some big guns on board, like Lord Peter Mandelson, Lord Wallace, Lord Wigley, and Baroness Rita Brady.

After mass resignations in September 2016 the company changes its name to Open Britain Ltd.

November 2015 - Four key negotiation points

Speaking at Chatham House, Cameron sets out the four key points that will form the basis of the negotiation with the EU.

'Today I am writing to the President of the European Council setting out how I want to address the concerns of the British people, and why I believe that the changes that Britain is seeking will benefit not just Britain, but the EU as a whole.'

In the letter to the President of the European Council Donald Tusk, PM David Cameron says that these four objectives lie at the heart of the UK's renegotiations:

➢ Protection of the single market for Britain and other non-euro countries

➢ Boosting competitiveness by setting a target to reduce the 'burden' of red tape

➢ Exempting Britain from 'ever-closer union' and bolstering national parliaments

➢ Restricting EU migrants' access to in-work benefits.

Former Tory Chancellor Lord Lawson comments that the four goals are 'disappointingly unambitious'.

Cameron may have set the bar low, but he has to get these points accepted by all 27 EU member states that have a bigger benefit from the status quo.

December 2015 - Donald Tusk on Cameron's letter

Council President Mr Donald Tusk writes a letter in preparation for a meeting in a week's time. It all looks pretty straightforward until you reach point four, 'the fourth basket', he writes:

'The fourth basket on social benefits and the free movement of persons is the most delicate and will require a substantive political debate at our December meeting. While we see good prospects for agreeing on ways to fight abuses and possibly on some reforms related to the export of child benefits, there is presently no consensus on the request that people coming to Britain from the EU must live there and contribute for four years before they qualify for in-work benefits or social housing. This is certainly an issue where we need to hear more from the British Prime Minister and an open debate among ourselves before proceeding further.'

'All in all, it is my assessment that so far we have made good progress. We need some more time to sort out the precise drafting on all of these issues, including the exact legal form the final deal will take. We also have to overcome the substantial political differences that we still have on the issue of social benefits and free movement.'

'The December European Council should address all the political dilemmas related to this process. Based on a substantive political discussion we should be able to prepare a concrete proposal to be finally adopted in February.'

December 2015 - Cameron visits Romania and Poland

Worried about a veto from Romania and Poland to his proposals to the European Council, Cameron visits the two countries who have expressed the most opposition to his plans as so many of their people migrate to the UK each year.

Cameron and the PM of Poland, Beata Szydlo, give a news conference after their talks. It sounds positive but when it comes to approval of his reforms, she doesn't support him.

17-18 December 2015 - EC summit in Brussels

There is no consensus at the summit for Cameron's watered down four-point plan. The main sticking point being the UK's wish to restrict access to benefits for new EU migrants.

MP Will Straw, executive director of Britain Stronger in Europe, tweets: 'The UK should continue to push for reform in Europe. British PMs have a strong track record of securing EU reform in the past.'

The recently appointed opposition Leader Jeremy Corbyn says migrants shouldn't need to wait for benefits: 'Cameron should seek fair rules on benefits that reflect the contributory principle, stop the undercutting of wages and protect the 'going rate' paid to skilled workers, and secure extra support, directly from the EU, for public services in the areas most affected by rapid change.'

'...Labour backs Britain's continued membership of the EU as the best framework for trade and cooperation in a 21st-century Europe. And we will campaign for Britain to stay when the referendum is finally held.'

'But people across Britain and Europe know that the EU needs to change if it's going to work better for the majority of its people, not just its banks and corporations.'

He goes on: 'Labour will be pressing for democratic reform to make EU decision making accountable to its people, economic reform to put jobs and sustainable growth at the centre of European policy, labour market reform to strengthen workers' rights in a real social Europe and new rights for elected authorities across Europe...'

December 2015 - Lively debate on EU pros and cons

Held at Oxford University; it's time to get informed.

Proposition (Remain) opens with Anne Williamson
Opposition (Leave) Jan Nedvidek
Proposition José Manuel Barroso, former EC President
Opposition Sir William Cash MP
Proposition Nick Clegg MP, former deputy PM
Opposition Nigel Farage MEP leader of the Brexit Party

Feb. 2016 - Cameron gets Polish and Danish backing

After the defeat at the December EC summit, he visits Poland again and Denmark. Cameron is making an all-out effort to convince them to stand with him on his proposals. He comes away confident that they will back him when it comes to a vote.

Speaking in London the President of the European Parliament, Martin Schultz, says, 'European leaders in Brussels, Luxembourg and Strasbourg are growing tired of British boat-rocking so, if Brits want to leave, let them leave.'

18-19 February 2016 - Deal struck by EC

Cameron and Donald Tusk, President of the European Council. come out of the EC summit triumphant, announcing a legally binding and irreversible deal signed by all 28 leaders. The deal addresses all of Cameron's concerns about remaining in the EU. Was it the deal Cameron really wanted?

Tusk says that the decision now lies with the British people. None of this was ever put into UK legislation.

'I deeply believe that the UK needs Europe, and Europe needs the UK. To break the link now would be totally against our mutual interests. We have done all we could not to let that happen.'

20 February 2016 - Cameron speaks in front of No.10

Cameron believes he can create a reformed European Union and announces that the referendum will be held on 23 June 2016. He is using language to scare the public with statements like, 'Those who want to leave Europe cannot tell you if businesses can access Europe's free trade single market'. I hear, if Britain leaves then, all trade with the EU will be blocked.

You don't always get what you want. Or do you?

The 23 June 2016 is the date set for Britain's second referendum concerning EU membership in over 40 years. The basis of the referendum is to renegotiate the UK's relationship with the EU and then to give the people the option to remain with a negotiated deal or to leave. Cameron has renegotiated but, for all the bravado, does the deal fall short of what he was asking for? His Chatham House speech laid out in detail what he wanted. After the deal, he feels confident enough to say it is giving the United Kingdom 'special status within the European Union' and he recommends the country vote Remain in four months' time. Let's take a look at the draft proposals.

Economic Governance

There are 'reassurances' that decisions will not be made favouring eurozone members over non-eurozone countries. It goes further to say non-eurozone countries will not be required to contribute to bailouts for eurozone countries.

In view of how easily the EP annulled the Irish referendum, are 'reassurances' really enough? I honestly think that when push comes to shove the EU will always protect its own interests first. The phrase Cameron used when the eurozone crisis first hit was: 'This deal is not in Britain's best interest.' so, he vetoed the deal. The EC simply went over his head doing it anyway risking devaluing the value of the pound.

Competitiveness

In this 'basket' there was a clear statement from the EU: 'The relevant EU institutions and the Member States will make all efforts to strengthen the internal market and to adapt it to keep pace with the changing environment.' This all makes good sense and the EU have been working tirelessly on this issue for many years.

Sovereignty

The proposal states: 'It is recognized that the United Kingdom, in the light of the specific situation it has under the treaties, is not committed to further political integration into the European Union. The substance of this will be incorporated into the treaties at the time of their next revision in accordance with the relevant provisions of the treaties and the respective constitutional requirements of the Member States, so as to make it clear that the references to ever closer union do not apply to the United Kingdom.' Could it be more vague?

A 'red-card' system is proposed that would allow a member of the Council, with the support of 15 other members (there are only 28 in all), to return a recommendation to the European Parliament for further changes to any policy. This is not a veto, as MEPs could still go ahead if they believe that they have addressed the concerns raised by the 'red card'. The 'yellow card' already exists and has only ever been used twice; an 'orange card' has never been used.

Social benefits and free movement

Member States, including the UK, could request (only once) an 'emergency brake' to limit access to in-work benefits for new arrivals from another named EU State. In the event a particular EU State experiences a mass exodus of people, a request could be put to the EP for approval, which they have the option to refuse. The emergency brake can be kept in place for a maximum period of seven years.

If, for example, 1.3 million people suddenly arrive in your country, it's too late to put such a plan in place as there is no mention of it being backdated. Also, the 'Visegrád Four' - the Czech Republic, Hungary, Poland and Slovakia – could veto it with QMV. Remember how voting in the Eurovision goes?

Wording will be changed with regard to deportation from 'does' to 'likely to' cause a threat.

No change is made to the principle of claiming child benefit for children residing elsewhere. However, adjustments can be made in the amount paid to reflect the difference in spending power in the country it is to be paid to. This is so vague that any court would overturn it.

In an attempt to curb sham marriages to gain EU access, legislation will be made to limit the ability of a non-EU national to gain the right to live and work in the EU. Any such law will certainly be challenged in the Court of Human Rights and most likely be overturned.

Is this a great deal?

Compared to Cameron's November 2014 list of nine 'tough new measures' (see page 195), his Chatham House speech lists a very watered-down version. Even this 'disappointingly unambitious' version is contested by Tusk. I believe the referendum should never have gone ahead on the basis of this negotiation as it didn't tick off Cameron's list as made clear during his Chatham House speech.

> ### So, the referendum now reads:
> ### Remain on a half-baked deal or Leave.

This is an important point because there are those who will vote Leave anyway, and those who will vote Remain regardless. The undecided will now be tempted to vote Leave, some with the notion that if the Leave vote wins it will give Cameron leverage to renegotiate an even better deal.

> ## Were the British people properly informed?

May 2016 - A Remain flyer is sent to every household

The Government had embedded in the European Union Referendum Act 2015 the right to send a 'guide' to every household in the UK and Gibraltar. The leaflet is entitled 'Why the Government believes that voting to remain in the European Union is the best decision for the UK' and states: 'This is your decision. The Government will implement what you decide'. This is in the week beginning 16 May 2016, at a cost of £9.3 million to the taxpayer, under the guise that the Government had a public duty to inform.

The leaflet states:

The UK has secured a special status in a reformed EU:

➢ we will not join the eurozone

➢ we will keep our own border controls

➢ UK won't be part of further European political integration

➢ there will be tough new restrictions on access to our welfare system for new EU migrants

➢ we have a commitment to reduce EU red tape

This leaflet sets out the facts, and explains why the Government believes a vote to remain in the EU is in the best interests of the people of the UK.

Cameron uses taxpayers' money to sway public opinion to vote Remain in a national referendum. And it's legal as the

House had passed legislation making it so. Why do Leave MPs sign off on this? Because it is presented to Parliament as a 'guide' to inform and not as a propaganda sheet for Remain.

June 2016 - In or Out?

> **In the week leading up to the Referendum, ALL polls give a majority of 2 to 4% for Remain**

Two and a half years have gone by since Cameron's 'Britain and Europe' speech on 23 January 2013 announcing a referendum. It has allowed plenty of time for the public to weigh up all the facts. There are lots of lively debates, and each side spent £7 million on campaigning, on top of the Government's 'informative' flyer. Cameron believes he has negotiated a deal that the public will be happy with.

In the lead-up to the referendum, all political parties without exception root for Remain. The BBC and the majority of UK news media show an obvious bias toward Remain.

> **The cards are heavily stacked in favour of Remain**

I personally thought the question on the referendum ballot was really simple, not at all ambiguous, with no conditions attached but lots of consequences. It made perfect sense...

'A ddylai'r Deyrnas Unedig aros yn aelod o'r Undeb
Ewropeaidd neu adael yr Undeb Ewropeaidd?'

The Welsh version was only used in Wales, in the UK it reads:

'Should the United Kingdom remain a member of the European Union or leave the European Union?'

The official Leave group, led by UKIP and such leaders as Johnson, Gove, Fox, Davis, and Rees-Mogg, are clearly the underdogs when it comes to clout. Funds for campaigning are limited to £7 million and few national newspapers support them. They nevertheless put up a fairly good fight. In my opinion, not such a great campaign and certainly not one that deserves to win.

The then Mayor of London, Boris Johnson, has to do a lot of soul searching before deciding which camp he's in, saying in February 2016, it is an 'agonisingly difficult decision': 'I want a better deal for the people of this country to save the money and to take back control. That's really what this is all about..'

The British public are enthusiastic, with reports of some 2.6 million people registering to vote in the final month.

As most people really don't understand what the debacle is about, what are they basing their vote on? Could it be that personalities and the trustworthiness of the main players are the biggest influences on the result?

Thursday 23 June 2016 - Britain votes Out

Leave vote wins by 1,269,528 votes, a lead of 3.78%

33,577,342 people vote, from a potential 46,500,001.

There's no point in discussing who voted, what age they were, and least of all which social class, after the horse has bolted. An unusually high turnout of 72.2% says public engagement was high. Some explanation for the unexpected end result may lie in the scare tactics of the Remain camp backfiring, together with no real solution being offered for the migration problem and the £350 million a week EU payments on the bus. Anyway,
... Strike Three!

The very next day, Cameron gives his final speech and resigns. Exerts from his speech:

'Good morning everyone, the country has just taken part in a giant democratic exercise, perhaps the biggest in our history. Over 33 million people from England, Scotland, Wales, Northern Ireland and Gibraltar have all had their say.'

'We should be proud of the fact that in these islands we trust the people for these big decisions.'

'We not only have a parliamentary democracy, but on questions about the arrangements for how we've governed there are times when it is right to ask the people themselves and that is what we have done.'

'The British people have voted to leave the European Union and their will must be respected.'

'I want to thank everyone who took part in the campaign on my side of the argument, including all those who put aside party differences to speak in what they believe was the national interest and let me congratulate all those who took part in the Leave campaign for the spirited and passionate case that they made.'

'The will of the British people is an instruction that must be delivered. It was not a decision that was taken lightly, not least because so many things were said by so many different organisations about the significance of this decision.'

'So there can be no doubt about the result. Across the world people have been watching the choice that Britain has made...'

'...I held nothing back, I was absolutely clear about my belief that Britain is stronger, safer and better off inside the European Union and I made clear the referendum was about this and this alone – not the future of any single politician including myself.'

'But the British people have made a very clear decision to take a different path and as such I think the country requires fresh leadership to take it in this direction.'

'I will do everything I can as prime minister to steady the ship over the coming weeks and months but I do not think it would be right for me to try to be the captain that steers our country to its next destination.'

'A negotiation with the European Union will need to begin under a new prime minister and I think it's right that this new prime minister takes the decision about when to trigger Article 50 and start the formal and legal process of leaving the EU. The British people have made a choice that not only needs to be respected but those on the losing side of the argument – myself included – should help to make it work.'

'Britain is a special country - we have so many great advantages - a parliamentary democracy where we resolve great issues about our future through peaceful debate, a great trading nation with our science and arts, our engineering and our creativity, respected the world over. And while we are not perfect, I do believe we can be a model for the multi-racial, multi-faith democracy, that people can come and make a contribution and rise to the very highest that their talent allows.'

'Although leaving Europe was not the path I recommended, I am the first to praise our incredible strengths. I said before that Britain can survive outside the European Union and indeed that we could find a way.'

'Now the decision has been made to leave, we need to find the best way and I will do everything I can to help.'

BOOK THREE

THE BREXIT BETRAYAL

(2016 - 2020)

INTRODUCTION

The People Have Spoken

Forty years of successive prime ministers talking about European Union reforms that never materialized, is probably a major factor in bringing about the 2016 referendum result.

So, the people have spoken.

In a democracy, that usually counts for something, or it used to. Doesn't the UK pride itself on upholding democracy? I'm therefore embarrassed that I have to define the word to plug a fundamental deficit in the UK education system.

Democracy is a Greek concept (δημοκρατία/dēmokratía) that literally means 'rule by the people'.

Then there's EU Democracy, which is fundamentally different. Yes, there's voting (but not as we know it Jim), for example, there's only ever one candidate on the ballot paper.

This reminds me of an interview some years back with the President of Egypt, the late dictator Hosni Mubarak who ruled between 1981-2011, when he said, 'In Egypt we have democracy, you can either vote for me or not' (only his name appeared on the ballot paper). He said this with the absolute conviction that he was giving democracy to Egypt.

We've seen other examples of EU-Democracy, such as when the European Parliament (EP) voted not to recognize the result of the Irish referendum in 2008, or when the European Council went over the head of David Cameron creating a situation that was potentially detrimental to Britain during the debt crisis. The EU try to legitimize actions that are undemocratic in the true sense of the word by calling it EU-Democracy.

Without doubt those who voted Remain felt an incredible sense of loss when the result was announced. After all, the majority of Parliamentarians and the leadership favoured Remain and the polls backed them up. The shock went deep and there had to be a simple explanation for why the country 'got it wrong'.

Some refuse to respect the 2016 referendum and are desperately trying to find ways to nullify it. This is practising EU Democracy by seeking ways to enforce a legitimate reversal.

Denial

Remainers try to take control of the narrative by crying out that the Leavers didn't know what they were voting for.

Were you properly informed? You have a responsibility to get yourself informed and not to rely solely on the salesperson. If you can't answer these three simple questions about the EU then I'm sorry, regardless of which camp you're in, your in or out decision was not an informed one.

Q1: Who is the President of the European Parliament?

Q2: Which political party is connected to the Europarty ECR?

Q3: How many UK referendums on the EU have been held?

And it is not realistic to say you're voting for the status quo, since EU policy is constantly evolving.

Anger

Many Remainers began to demand a second referendum.

In order to have a second referendum, the first one must be either executed or annulled by legislation in Parliament. Some say that a second referendum would achieve the same result. Would that result then be respected?

Why not make it best out of three when voting for MPs? After all, people are allowed to change their minds - and probably don't know who they're voting for anyway.

It boils down to what Remain MPs are planning

Drag out and frustrate the Brexit process to a point where the general public will agree to anything just to make it go away.

The seven years of hell continues...

Bargaining

Remember the extension, the extension, and the extension?

Do you remember what the referendum was based on?

Cameron's attempt to negotiate a better deal had failed.

The Leave vote wasn't just saying 'Leave', it was also rejecting the negotiated deal.

Depression

The NHS has already had a conference on the negative mental state of young people due to a long drawn-out Brexit.

Acceptance

It will take some years before many people in Britain reach this stage.

An insight to the EU

The EU is simply a club for countries that happen to be located next to one another. They are not friends; they are more like work colleagues. Each country looks out for its own interests and makes sure it squeezes as much as it can out of the club. EU member states cannot work on a level playing field and, due to their economic differences, probably never will. Richer countries (such as Germany, Britain, and France) all contribute far more to the EU than they will ever get out of it; and poorer countries (such as the Visegrád Four) will need support for many years to come. Then there's Greece, who sees the EU as a never-ending stream of free money. But they pay interest I hear you say. So far this has been paid as part the next tranche of bailout funds so, technically, Greece has never actually paid any interest.

Many Brits believe that other EU member states think as we do and have the same economic standards. Sorry, but anyone who has travelled knows this is simply not the case.

One of the biggest differences lies in the state pensions. Here's a chart showing what people get as a percentage of their final salary in EU member states. The UK is in last place, with pensioners receiving 29% of their last wage, on average.

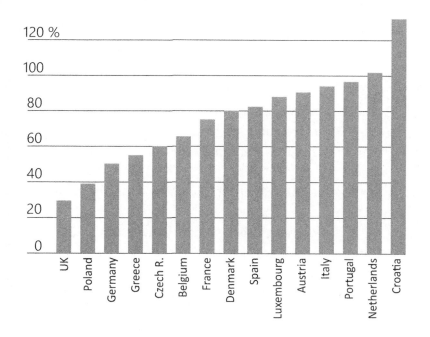

Will the UK lose out on free trade?

Studies on tariffs in the 1960s concluded that import/export duties cost more in administration than they generate in revenues. Today, tariffs are used to protect industries from other countries dumping goods too cheaply - for example, China's cheap steel, which has bankrupted most steel plants in Europe because governments acted too late.

If tariffs were introduced between the UK and EU, then Britain would receive a net benefit of around £5.6 billion per year, due to the UK importing more than she exports. This could be used to subsidize important sectors.

➢ UK exports 2018 to EU: £289bn (46% of all UK exports)

➢ UK imports 2018 from EU: £345bn (54% of all UK imports)

➢ Total trade deficit 2018 with the EU: -£56bn

➢ UK has a trade surplus of £44bn with non-EU countries

The EU sells £56 billion worth of goods to the UK more than the UK exports, and the UK pays the EU a membership fee of around £1 billion per month for this privilege.

On tariffs, the EU will certainly want a deal quickly

The EU treated the UK like a rich relative, until Margaret Thatcher put a stop to the unfair practice of excessive CAP payments. Is Britain getting good value for money? Let's apply some common sense. The £1 billion a month paid to the EU that, among other things, helps Eastern Bloc countries get on their feet (creating a future market for richer EU states) could be better spent in the UK. In 2018 a net payment of £15.5 billion in real money, after the rebate, was transferred from the UK to the EU.

Let me put it another way. It's like going to a supermarket and paying £5 at a turnstile for the privilege of shopping there. In addition, this supermarket will dictate who you can talk to and shop with. If you want to shop next door you must pay the supermarket a percentage of anything you buy there. Read the section on CAP page 24.

EU market access only with freedom of movement?

Access to the EU's single market is already enjoyed by 165 countries with no requirement for freedom of movement of people. Both Canada (CETA) and Japan have EU free trade agreements, without the free movement of people.

Juncker and Tusk are very clear, unless the UK allows freedom of movement of people there will be tariffs on exports to the EU. They often mention the four freedoms (free movement of goods, capital, labour, and services).

The EU feels that they have no choice but to punish the UK for leaving and believes scare tactics will encourage Britain to stay. They must set an example to deter other member states from even considering leaving.

Upon leaving, the minimum wage may be unnecessary. It was in direct response to the influx of EU migrants. Taking back control of borders means the downward pressure on pay for low-skilled jobs will cease and wages for young people could well pick up.

I look forward to seeing responsible reporting in the press. A scare mongering, biased media have been making buzz words out of phrases like crashing out and falling off a cliff. When sensationalism is used over a long period it has an effect on the mental wellbeing of many people.

What are the consequences of Brexit on the EU?

The loss of Britain's net contribution (£15.5 billion in 2018) will cause the biggest headache by far as only Germany and France are in a position to help make up the shortfall. But since mid-2018 Germany has shown signs of an economic slowdown. German MEP Hans-Olaf Henkel says that the UK leaving is equivalent to 19 smaller countries leaving.

The UK is the fifth-largest economy in the world and the second-largest in the EU

This fact should never be underestimated when it comes to how important UK market access is for the EU, and especially for the poorer countries.

Britain is seen as an ally by France and Germany when voting on policy in the EP. After the UK leaves, qualified majority voting (QMV) puts Germany and France in a weaker position for pushing policy through and there is a risk of the Mediterranean countries or the Eastern Bloc coming together to push through policies that work in their favour.

The risk of other member states deciding to leave and causing a collapse like a house of cards is another worrying factor. There are only a handful of member states whose economy could withstand an exit from the EU.

Brexit is a man-made problem, it is not some meteorite hurtling toward the planet over which we have no control. Where there's a will, there's a way. The consequences of a hard Brexit as portrayed by the press, such as trucks queuing for 50 miles outside Dover, do not take into account the other side of the channel. We should not underestimate the bloody mindedness of the French to ensure there are ques of lorries leading to Dover.

Poland is the largest beneficiary of EU funds receiving €105.8bn from 2014 to 2020. This has helped them catch up with the West, achieving 5.0% growth in 2018. There will come a point when people will earn more in Poland than in the UK. The Polish economy can be regarded as stable. It exported about £12.88 billion worth of goods to the UK in 2018, so a blockade at Calais of just four weeks would lose Poland £1,000,000,000 in trade. The economy might be stable, but such a situation could collapse many companies in Poland, with a devastating effect on the Polish economy.

CHAPTER EIGHT

Brexit Means Brexit

July 2016 - Theresa May in charge in under 3 weeks

As David Cameron resigns, Theresa May, a Remainer, wins against three experienced Brexit MPs to become the second female British prime minister on 13 July 2016. Right from the start she coins the phrase, 'Brexit means Brexit'. She creates a Cabinet in which three-quarters are Remainers.

With 330 seats in Parliament, she thinks she has a good chance of pushing policy through. She immediately assigns the job of Brexit Secretary to David Davis MP, who was Europe Minister. Boris Johnson becomes Foreign Secretary.

Despite holding a majority in the House of Commons, Theresa May finds it impossible to push through any Brexit deal. The problems that a mostly Remain Parliament causes her are, I'm sure in part, the reason that Cameron quit his post. The real problem is highlighted in the maps over the page. The people voted leave but the politicians didn't!

As we have seen, PM May has a very good hand with which to negotiate a deal with the EU, who has more to lose if the end solution is no-deal. Remember, the world is still hurting from a financial crisis that affected the UK less than most EU states, partly because it was not in the eurozone. Sensible housekeeping by the UK Government and timely reactions from the Bank of England all contributed to the UK doing OK.

Comparing debt to GDP ratios indicates a country's financial standing. In 2016, Germany's debt to GDP ratio was 60.9%, France's 98.4%, Italy's 132.2%, and the UK's 86.8%. Germany therefore has the least amount of debt.

If you remember, in 1979 the UK had a debt to GDP ratio of only 44.55%, which was considered a big problem as interest rates of over 10% were very high. Low interest rates mean cheaper borrowing for governments, so the 2016 ratios are not so problematic, on condition interest rates remain low.

Slovakia, with a debt to GDP ratio of 49%, Romania with 36%, the Czech Republic with 32.75%, and Poland with 49%, all have much less debt than the West. So why is the EU still handing over billions in 'modernization' funds?

If Britain stops paying the one billion pounds per month to the EU it would go a long way to reducing the UK's national debt of more than double that of those 'poor' countries who receive massive EU funding.

But, I digress. With a public that voted 'Leave' and a House of Commons that voted 'Remain' the country has a dilemma.

HOW CONSTITUENCIES VOTED IN THE 2016 REFERENDUM

HOW MPs VOTED IN THE 2016 REFERENDUM

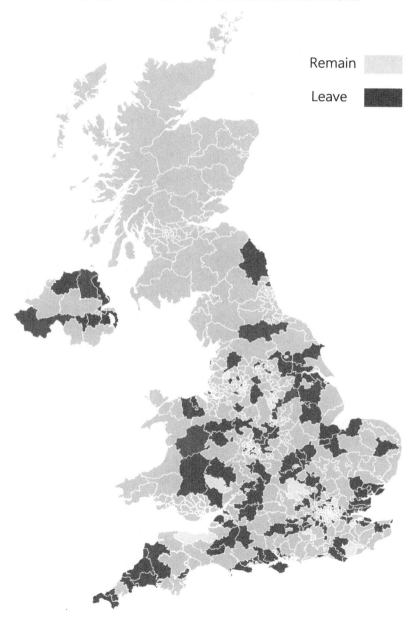

Remain

Leave

Comparison of the two maps highlights how many MPs representing Leave constituencies voted Remain and vice versa. The country has a situation whereby elected lawmakers are clearly not in agreement with voters. Is the job of an MP to do the will of the people or what they consider to be best?

If the referendum is considered on a constituency basis, which is how it's calculated in elections, then the Leave result is overwhelming, with 406 voting Leave and 242 Remain. With two-thirds of UK constituencies voting Leave, consider how this could be translated in a general election.

The 2016 referendum (which cost £129 million) is 'advisory', which means that the Government has no obligation whatsoever to act on it. At the Conservative Party Conference on 2 October 2016, Prime Minister May announces a repeal of the European Communities Act 1972 saying she will trigger Article 50, as required by the Lisbon Treaty. She goes on to say that she will go for a 'hard' Brexit if that is the only option to end the free movement of people from the EU. She says;

'We are facing a moment of great change as a nation. As we leave the European Union, we must define an ambitious new role for ourselves in the world. That involves asking ourselves what kind of country we want to be: a confident, global trading nation that continues to play its full part on the world stage.'

'But at the same time, I believe I have a precious opportunity to step back and ask some searching questions about what kind of country we want to be here at home too.'

'In fact, it's not just an opportunity, but a duty. Because one thing is clear. When the British people voted in the referendum, they did not just choose to leave the European Union. They were also expressing a far more profound sense of frustration about aspects of life in Britain and the way in which politics and politicians have failed to respond to their concerns.'

'Some voted for the first time in more than 30 years. Some for the first time ever. And they were inspired to do so because they saw a chance to reject the politics of 'business as usual' and to demand real, profound change.'

'Fed up with being ignored or told that their priorities were somehow invalid, based on ignorance and misunderstanding, or even on occasion that they were simply wrong to voice the concerns that they did, they took their opportunity to send a very clear message: they will not be ignored any more!'

'They want to take back control of the things that matter in their lives. They want a government that listens, understands and is on their side. They want change. And this government is going to deliver it'.

October 2016 - Gina Miller got it right

The millionaire and activist Gina Miller argues in court (R. Miller v Secretary of State for Exiting the European Union) that the Government cannot trigger Article 50 without approval from Parliament and that only Parliament can take away rights that Parliament has granted.

On 3 November 2016 the court rules in her favour, that Parliament has to legislate before Article 50 can be triggered. May's Government appeals directly to the Supreme Court, who deliver their judgement in January 2017, upholding the High Court ruling by a majority of 8-3.

In effect, Gina Miller has taken an advisory referendum and forced Parliament to make it a legally binding undertaking by the Government to trigger Article 50. Regardless of how much you may disagree with it, only Parliament is sovereign, and Miller's questioning was right. This is taking back power by allowing our own courts to decide.

When people now ask if it was legal to trigger Article 50, the answer is simply yes, as Parliament created the legislation.

THE BOTTOM LINE

Parliament approves triggering Article 50

The House of Commons votes 498 to 114, and the House of Lords votes 274 to 118 in favour of passing the Brexit bill (Notification of Withdrawal), which becomes law on 16 March 2017.

---

28 October 2016 - The High Court in Northern Ireland rules in favour of the UK Government, saying that they do not require the consent of the Northern Ireland Assembly to leave the EU.

Theresa May's statement at the EC summit

October 2016, Theresa May attends her first European Council summit. In a press conference afterwards she says, 'The UK is leaving the EU, but we are not leaving Europe - and we are not turning our backs on our friends and allies.'

'While we have not yet formally started the exit negotiations, here at this summit I have been clear that my aim is to cement Britain as a close partner of the EU once we have left.'

'Yes, the United Kingdom will be a fully independent, sovereign country, free to make our own decisions on a whole host of different issues, such as how we choose to control immigration.'

November 2016 - PM Szydło at No. 10

PM Theresa May meets with the Polish prime minister and a statement at the end makes some very important points.

The Polish PM says, 'We want to make sure that as part of the negotiations, the guarantees are maintained for the Polish citizens who live and work in the United Kingdom.'

May says, 'Since we last met in July, the UK has made significant progress to prepare for the negotiations and I will trigger Article 50 before the end of March next year.'

'I have also reiterated my plan to guarantee the rights of Poles and other Europeans currently living in the UK, so long as the rights of British citizens living across the EU are guaranteed.'

December 2016 - EU plans are leaked

A leaked document reveals the tone of EU negotiations with regard to the UK and how directives from the European Commission are sidestepping the European Parliament. It says: Juncker will act as chief negotiator; a hardline stance will be taken; access to the single market requires acceptance of all four freedoms, which includes the free movement of people.

January 2017 - Negotiation objectives

Theresa May gives a speech at Lancaster House, where Margaret Thatcher announced her support for a single European market 29 years earlier. May sets out a 12-point plan that amounts to one big goal: a new, positive, and constructive partnership between Britain and the European Union. Her message to the four nations of the United Kingdom is that she wants a smooth and orderly Brexit.

PMQs after the speech

PMQs on 18 January highlight the differences between the political parties as to how Britain will negotiate an exit from the EU, and the problems to come.

February 2017 - Government White Paper

Theresa May and her Government publish a White Paper called, 'The United Kingdom's exit from, and new partnership with, the European Union'. It sets out proposals for future legislation and confirms details of the prime minister's 12 principles from her speech in January.

Parliament creates legislation so May can trigger Article 50 voting 498 to 114. MPs are subdued and not cheering at the result as so many of them voted Remain in the referendum.

The EU nominates the Commission as the organization within the union responsible for negotiations and appoints Michel Barnier as chief negotiator. Acting on a mandate from the EU27 leaders, he will negotiate and report back to the Council (EC).

March 2017 - Article 50 Triggered

Parliamentary legislation allows PM May to trigger Article 50. On 29 March 2017 she gives formal notification to the EU in a letter handed to the European Council President, Donald Tusk, by Sir Tim Barrow, the UK's permanent representative in Brussels. There's now no turning back. Once triggered, Article 50 cannot be unilaterally reversed. This marks the beginning of a two-year countdown to leaving.

Tusk, now starting his second term as Council President says, 'I personally wish the UK hadn't chosen to leave the EU, but the majority of British voters decided otherwise. Therefore, we must do everything we can to make the process of divorce the least painful for the EU.' He is obviously personally touched and practically in tears as he speaks to the press.

Within 48 hours of receiving formal notification, Tusk issues guidelines for the Brexit talks and calls the European Council (in an EU27 format, without the UK) to a meeting on Saturday 29 April 2017 to adopt his guidelines.

The Tusk guidelines are tough and reinforce the EU policy that any deal to include access to the single market is impossible without acceptance of the four freedoms (free movement of goods, capital, labour, and services). They state that there can be no cherry-picking with regard to the four freedoms. Here are some of the stipulations in Tusk's guidelines:

1. The European Council welcomes the recognition by the British Government that the four freedoms of the single market are indivisible and that there can be no cherry-picking.

2. In accordance with the principle that nothing is agreed until everything is agreed, individual items cannot be settled separately.

24. After the United Kingdom leaves the Union, no agreement between the EU and the UK will apply to the territory of Gibraltar without an agreement between the Kingdom of Spain and the United Kingdom.
The guide goes on to talk about a single financial settlement,

which the press refers to as the divorce bill. It should be pointed out that no actual sum of money is ever mentioned.

Nigel Farage gives his opinion about the guidelines to the EU Parliament calling them a serious of unreasonable demands and comparing them to the Mafia.

April 2017 - Theresa May calls a snap election

The prime minister Theresa May is faced with a Parliament and a House of Lords that threaten to sabotage every effort she makes toward Brexit. They openly vow to fight her every step of the way, which creates deadlock.

She gives an emotional and sombre speech in front of 10 Downing Street: 'The country is coming together but Westminster is not. In recent weeks Labour have threatened to vote against the final agreement we reach with the European Union. The Liberal Democrats have said they want to grind the business of government to a standstill. The Scottish National Party say they will vote against the legislation that formally repeals Britain's membership of the European Union, and unelected members of the House of Lords have vowed to fight us every step of the way.'

The next scheduled general election should take place on 7 May 2020, she has little alternative but to call an early election on 8 June 2017. She believes that a fresh mandate from the British people will strengthen her hand at the negotiating table. The Fixed-term Parliaments Act 2011, introduced by David Cameron's coalition, specifies the conditions under which an election can be called: in the first instance, an election is scheduled for the first Thursday in May of the fifth year that a government has been in office; or when two-thirds of MPs in the House of Commons agree a motion to hold an election; or when a sitting prime minister loses a vote of no confidence and no alternative government is confirmed by the Commons within 14 days.

MPs vote in favour of an early general election by 522 to 13, this fulfils the two-thirds majority condition.

April 2017 - EU27 discuss negotiation guidelines

The EU27 unanimously endorse the Tusk Draft guidelines on 29 April 2017 just 15 minutes into the meeting. They agree a phased approach, with the first phase focusing on:

➢ guarantee EU and UK citizen's rights

➢ settle the UK's financial obligations to the EU

➢ avoid a hard border between Ireland and Northern Ireland.

At the top of their agenda is protecting the rights of the 3.4 million EU citizens living in the UK. Especially those from Eastern Bloc countries, as the workers' remittances and family allowance payments are crucial to millions of families back home. To this end the guidelines go further and request the right to a UK passport after a continuous residency of five years (Germany requires a residency of seven years).

The EU believes that the UK should make a financial settlement to leave, although UK contributions over the years have helped poorer member states grow, and the UK will never see a return from that investment. The initial figure was around €60 billion but no actual basis is given for how this amount is arrived at.

There will be a financial shortfall to the EU budget when the UK leaves, but richer member states refuse to pay more and poorer states, led by Poland, do not want to receive less. The UK has signed an obligation to continue payments (circa £1 billion per month) to the EU budget, ending in 2020. The EU has no plans to reduce future spending, despite the projected shortfall.

In view of Ireland's ambitions for Irish reunification, the guidelines refer to the Good Friday Agreement (GFA) 'in all its parts'. In the event that a referendum held in Northern Ireland votes in favour of reunification then they will automatically become part of the EU. There is no suggestion on how to avoid a hard border, and the free movement of goods will continue as is called for in the GFA.

Scotland with ambitions to break away from the UK are not given any such assurance of EU membership in the future.

238 ◆ The Brexit Betrayal

June 2017 - May's minority Government

The snap election on 8 June 2017 is a disaster and leaves the Conservatives nine seats short of the 326 required to form a majority. Having lost 13 seats PM May must now consider with whom she could form a coalition Government.

The biggest winner is Jeremy Corbyn as Labour gain 30 seats across the country, now with a total of 262.

The SNP campaigned on Scottish independence and on protecting Scotland's interests in the Brexit negotiations. They lose 21 seats, ending up with just 35 - a dozen of those lost seats go to Conservatives. Their commanding majority in the 2015 elections of 56 out of 59 seats in Scotland is short lived. This doesn't make calls for another referendum any less likely.

Back in April the polls showed an enthusiastic 21-point lead in favour of a Conservative win, which is one of the main reasons May called the election when she did.

The attempt to 'strengthen her hand' and 'secure a Brexit mandate' backfires as it results in a hung parliament. The Conservatives win the popular vote by 42.4% to Labour's 40%, with a turnout of 68.8%, although May had dodged debates and was noticeably out of the public eye in the run up. An unpopular social care shake-up the press branded 'the dementia tax', and Labour's resolution to mobilize younger voters with Corbyn's bold promises of ,free universities', contribute to May losing the majority she'd inherited.

Theresa May maintains power by joining forces with the Northern Irish Democratic Unionist Party (DUP) led by Arlene Foster, who supports a 'hard' Brexit. They only have ten seats, giving the coalition a one seat majority leaving the Conservatives in a weaker position than before the election. The coalition with the DUP changes the dynamics of the Brexit negotiations in view of the complexities of the Irish border and the DUP's hard stance on the EU.

'This government will guide the country through the crucial Brexit talks and deliver on the will of the British people by taking the United Kingdom out of the European Union.' May said.

Has this election solved the basic problem Theresa May faced when she first announced it, that Parliament are fighting against leaving the EU at all cost.

If Labour or the Lib-Dems had won this election, we would have seen a complete reversal of Brexit on the spot.
... **Strike Four!**

June 2017 - Withdrawal talks begin

Michel Barnier and UK negotiator David Davis meet face to face for the first formal talks in the European Commission's headquarters on 19 June 2017. They seem very positive on day one that a deal is possible and that it would be far better than no deal.

Talks on a withdrawal agreement focus on: 'lifting the uncertainty' for EU citizens living in the UK and Brits living in the EU; a financial settlement; and the issue of the Irish border. There is a separate negotiating team for each issue. Barnier insists that no trade talks can begin until these three issues have been fully addressed.

David Davis after one year in the job resigns and is replaced by Dominic Raab July 2018; Raab only lasts four months and leaves just before the breakthrough. On 14 November 2018 a 599-page draft withdrawal agreement is presented.

On the three main issues it states

➢ rights of those already living in the EU/UK are guaranteed

➢ UK to honour funding to 2020 with a single settlement

➢ the Northern Ireland Protocol avoids a hard border.

A statement from Siegfried Muresan MEP (Romania EPP group) explains that the EU budget needs to increase to give more money to British universities for research. He fails to understand Farage's explanation that the EU are only returning money Britain paid to the EU in the first place.

The Withdrawal Agreement is endorsed on 25 November 2018 by all 27 member states of the European Council.

An actual figure for a 'divorce bill' is nowhere to be found, although the House of Lords acknowledges that the EU may claim on previous obligations entered into by treaty. Amounts to be submitted for the 'divorce bill' have been estimated as between £30 billion and £200 billion. The Lords report also concludes that in the case of 'no-deal' the UK has no legal obligation to make any 'exit' payments to the EU.

When the deal is hailed by Theresa May as the deal that will please everybody -

- you just know it will end up pleasing nobody.

July 2017 - Cabinet hammer out the Chequers plan

The EU agrees that the second phase of negotiations can begin, that of future relationships. Differences within the Conservative party on the future of Brexit are to be ironed out on 6 July in a Cabinet meeting at Chequers (the country house used by a sitting prime minister). The plan that is supposed to make everybody happy causes the Brexit Secretary, David Davis, and the Foreign Secretary, Boris Johnson, to resign in opposition to it. Boris returns to the backbench. The Chequers plan lays out proposals for future relationships between the UK and the EU, for example, no hard border between Northern Ireland and Ireland. EU negotiator Michel Barnier and EU leaders dismiss the plan as unacceptable.

Proposals discussed at Chequers are never instigated.

June 2018 - European Union (Withdrawal) Act

This bill, introduced by David Davis, repeals the European Communities Act 1972 and additionally requires parliamentary approval for any withdrawal agreement negotiated with the EU. It passes through Parliament on 20 June 2018 and becomes law by Royal Assent on 26 June.

The Act makes ratification of any deal dependent upon the prior enactment of another Act of Parliament which must approve the final terms of withdrawal when negotiations are complete. On what was to become known as Super Saturday, 19 October 2019, Sir Oliver Letwin relies on this bill to delay a new deal by Boris Johnson until Parliament can pass the necessary law (the deal requires parliamentary approval) to enact the agreement.

December 2018 - May wins vote of no confidence

Parliament has concerns about the Withdrawal Agreement (the Brexit bill). PM May delays a vote in the House, takes the initiative and heads off to Brussels to secure further assurances on the Northern Ireland question. Juncker makes it very clear that this is the only deal and that no more negotiations will be held. She comes back with no concessions whatsoever.

On her return, Theresa May receives 48 letters from Tory Brexit hardliners challenging her position as party leader - losing a vote of no confidence can trigger an election. She fights back and wins the ballot by 200 votes to 117.

The Brexit bill - thrice failed - still going strong

On 19 January 2019 Parliament rejects the Withdrawal Agreement by a vote of 432 to 202. Corbyn calls a no-confidence vote for the next day. Tory MPs, worried about an election, rally round and May survives the motion of no confidence by 325 votes to 306. This is a close call.

A month later no fewer than eight Labour MPs resign to form The Independent Group (better known as Change UK), citing Labour as 'institutionally anti-Semitic' and 'complicit in facilitating Brexit'. Two days later they are joined by three Conservative MPs who believe that their party has become hostage to Brexit hardliners.

On 12 March 2019 Parliament rejects the Brexit deal yet again, 391 to 242 votes. The leave date is less than three weeks away so, Parliament also votes overwhelmingly to seek a delay to the March 29 deadline. A request for an extension requires the approval of all 27 EU member states. Accordingly, Theresa May writes to Donald Tusk on 20 March 2019 requesting the first extension for a period of three months to 30 June 2019. The EU agree a shorter extension to April 12.

Parliamentarians show how they can waste taxpayers' money and prove they can agree on nothing when it comes to Brexit. MPs take control of the House for three days to find some consensus in a series of 'indicative votes' but, as each result ends with the speaker of the House saying, 'the noes have it, the noes have it', it is all just a waste of time.

On 29 March 2019, UK law makers reject the Brexit deal for a third time, by 344 votes to 286.

THE BOTTOM LINE

Is the deal that's supposed to please everybody really that unacceptable or will Parliament only sign up to a deal that ends in a Remain result?

In January 2019 a non-binding amendment to prevent a no-deal Brexit, tabled by Remainer Caroline Spelman (Con), is approved by 318 votes to 310. Following months of death threats, she announces she will not seek re-election again.

February 2019 - Free trade agreement with Japan

The Economic Partnership Agreement (EPA) between Japan and the EU comes into force. It gives access to the single market. Can you move to Japan? No. It seems that the four freedoms concept does not apply to the Japanese, meaning they can cherry-pick whereas the UK cannot.

March 2019 - Londoner's march to stop Brexit

London voted overwhelmingly for remain in the referendum, which could explain the massive turnout to the Put It To The People march calling for a second referendum. Organizers claim that more than a million people turn out on 23 March.

April 2019 - Time to request another extension

The European Union (Withdrawal) Act 2019 is tabled by Yvette Cooper (Lab) and Sir Oliver Letwin (Con) on 3 April 2019 (Cooper–Letwin bill). The next day it's being debated by the House of Lords in a historically short legislative period. The bill to stop a no-deal Brexit and to force Theresa May to request an extension to at least 22 May 2019 is passed by both Houses in only three working days.

Again, Theresa May formally requests an extension to the exit date of 30 June 2019. EC members question why they should grant an extension that will require Britain to take part in the upcoming European elections and that will continue a state of uncertainty for all concerned. On 11 April 2019 the EC agree to a further extension to allow for the ratification of the Withdrawal Agreement bill (Brexit bill). Such an extension should last no longer than 31 October 2019.

EU members also say that if the UK refuses to take part in the forthcoming EU elections, the extension will cease with immediate effect. The UK remains a full member of the European Union until the day after exit day, now 1 November.

New Exit Date - 31 October 2019

The House of Lords are mostly Remainers and there are attempts to block Brexit by preventing bills from passing through the House. They are warned by Lord Michael Lord.

Easter Break recess: 11-23 April 2019

May Break recess: 2-7 May 2019

Despite PM May requesting an extension to Article 50 as Parliament has failed to find a consensus, no one thinks to table a motion to cancel any of the 29 days of holidays to continue their important work.

Theresa May offers to step down as prime minister and to hold a second referendum if Parliament agrees to pass the Brexit bill. Parliament refuses her offer.

Whitsun Break recess: 23 May-4 June 2019

23 May 2019 - European Parliamentary elections held

This is the election that was not supposed to happen as Britain should already be out of the EU. There's a turnout of only 37% and Farage's newly formed Brexit Party sweeps up, it takes 29 of the 73 seats. The Brexit Party gets 5,248,533 votes against the number two contender, the Lib-Dems, with 3,367,284 votes. A difference of 1,881,249.

I am absolutely dumbfounded and have to ask: Where are the now, very vocal Remainers who love the EU so much that they can't be bothered to get out and vote for their MEP? Nigel Farage's confidence and resolve shows in his speeches. **... Strike Five!**

7 June 2019 - PM Theresa May resigns

When the answer to signing her Brexit deal is still no, Theresa May announces her resignation on 7 June 2019. She will continue as caretaker PM until a successor is chosen.

24 July 2019 - Theresa May steps down

It has been a tenure of three long years, dominated by Brexit and fighting a mostly, Remain Parliament. She puts on a brave face to the very end. Her moving resignation speech in front of No. 10 shows her as a compassionate leader with many years of public service to the country she loves. Unfortunately, her legacy will be that, she failed to deliver on Brexit.

MPs are feeling chipper and believe that any old fool can be a prime minister. Ten MPs enter the leadership race for No. 10. Three fail to get the minimum support of eight other MPs (at this stage the minimum to stay in the race) and another quits, leaving six candidates to battle it out. Two of the hopefuls stemming from the 2016 leadership election, Michael Gove and Andrea Leadsom, throw their hats into the ring again.

The final choice though is to be decided between Boris Johnson (Brexiteer, former Foreign Secretary) and Jeremy Hunt (Remainer, Foreign Secretary).

When the vote is put to the 160,000 Conservative members, two-thirds vote in favour of Boris Johnson.

CHAPTER NINE

Get Brexit Done

July 2019 - Boris Johnson becomes prime minister

The new prime minister is not elected through a general election but by a postal ballot of the Conservative membership, with 138,800 casting their vote. It's the first time that a Brexiteer is at the helm, and the leading voice of the Leave campaign prior to the 2016 referendum. The man who's famous for dangling from a zip wire over the river Thames and who sometimes acts the clown, is now entrusted with getting Brexit done.

The referendum three years ago has not just polarized the nation, it's left everyone suffering from battle fatigue. Can the will of the people finally be carried out on Johnson's watch?

Johnson is a fairly experienced politician who is 55 when he accepts the position he has hankered after for such a long time. He unexpectedly ruled himself out of the leadership race in 2016, allowing his friend Michael Gove to carry the torch, who then lost to Theresa May.

Johnson was born in New York to upper-middle-class British parents. His father, Stanley, was employed by the European Commission (his wife's father was President of the European Commission of Human Rights at the time), so the family moved to Brussels in April 1973, where Boris and his three siblings learnt to speak French. Johnson suffered from deafness from an early age, for which he had surgery. He was awarded a King's Scholarship to study at Eton College from 1977 and became close friends with Charles Spencer (Princess Diana's brother). He received another scholarship to study Classics at Oxford University in late 1983.

Johnson's first real job is trainee at The Times newspaper, where he becomes a journalist, only to be sacked after falsely claiming that a certain quote came from his own godfather. Through a personal connection, he moves on to become a writer at the Daily Telegraph - it is said that Margaret Thatcher became a fan of his articles.

He decides on a career change and is elected Conservative MP for Henley following Michael Heseltine's retirement. He enters the House of Commons for the first time in 2001. He is already friends with Michael Gove, George Osborne, and David Cameron – his becoming an MP brings them closer.
In May 2008 he is elected Mayor of London. He holds

the office for eight years before returning to the House of Commons July 2016 as Foreign Secretary under Theresa May.

Three years later Boris Johnson wins the leadership race to inherit a party and a country deeply divided over the future. In his opening speech on 24 July 2019, in front of No. 10's famous black front door, PM Boris Johnson pledges that Britain will leave the EU on 31 October 2019, no ifs, no buts.

Johnson sets off for talks with the German Chancellor, Angela Merkel. She appears to set him a deadline of 30 days to find an alternative to the Irish backstop. The signs to date indicate that the deal on the table is the only deal, but Johnson is testing the ground to see how much scope there is for renegotiation.

Next day he's with the French President, Emmanuel Macron, who describes the Irish backstop as 'indispensable'.

If Boris wants to reopen negotiations, he needs the support of the two most powerful nations within the EU. There is a saying that when Merkel speaks, others listen. When Xi Jinping visits Europe in March 2019, who does he see? Italian Giuseppe Conte then Juncker, then Macron and Merkel, but not Sebastian Kurz, Mateusz Morawiecki, nor Pedro Sánchez. EU power lies clearly with Germany and France.

25 July 2019, Johnson's first House of Commons statement and taking questions from MPs about his vision of Brexit.
With Boris Johnson at the helm, the chances of a no-deal Brexit have been raised and, as the majority of MPs are opposed

to this, they start plotting ways to stop such a scenario. Boris seems resolute about coming out on 31 October, 'with or without a deal' - a phrase he repeats many times.

BBC presenter Gary Robertson first coins the phrase 'crashing out' if there is no deal. Other derogatory phrases used by a biased press to scare the public are 'cliff edge', 'hard Brexit', and 'Regrexit'. What if there's no deal?

Will there be food in the shops?

Only 28% of the UK's food requirements come from the EU. There's a wealth of partners eager to step in and feed the UK – and they are cheaper. The Commonwealth is alive and well and wants to do business with the UK.

All agreements between the UK and the EU have one thing in common, Juncker says, 'EU countries will not suffer due to Brexit'. Juncker might not care whether the UK starves but he must ensure that nothing detrimental happens to businesses in the EU. Will Juncker hinder Spain from selling their cucumbers? Will France let truckloads of goods pile up at Calais and block them from entering the UK? Common sense will prevail, and the Withdrawal Agreement is only about 'divorce' and not about the future relationship between the UK and the EU (which will take another few years of negotiations to complete).

Let's cut to the chase. We're talking about two economies trading in billions of pounds of business every single day. A no-deal scenario would motivate the EU to conclude a trade deal much more quickly and have them more likely to grant concessions. In reality, a no-deal would make the EU agree to a freeze and allow everything to continue until future treaties are negotiated (a transition period).

The EU want to fly their aeroplanes to the UK, and they want to sell their cars and services to the UK. After all, the UK is the EU's second-largest export market for goods, amounting to 18% of their total exports. This makes the UK not just important to the EU but also invaluable and indispensable – and this is why they're sad. Unfortunately, the biased British press only picture one side of the story, making the public believe that the EU holds all the cards and that food shortages will be the result of leaving.

Some food for thought

In 2017 the EU exports goods worth €375,826 billion to the USA - this includes goods worth €48 billion from the UK.

Top UK export products sold to the USA are:
vehicles ($11 bn), machinery ($9.3 bn), special other ($5.3 bn), pharmaceutical ($5.0 bn), and fuels ($4.3 bn).

In 2017 the EU exports goods worth €259,000 bn to the UK. This represents one billion euros per working day! Do they really want to mess that up?

August 2019 - Jeremy Corbyn's coup attempt

The majority of MPs on both sides of the House are opposed to Brexit and working very hard to stop it. They shudder at the very thought of a 'no-deal' Brexit openly admitting that they will fight tooth and nail against a 'no-deal'. Aware of public sentiment, a fight against a 'no-deal' sounds legitimate, but in actual fact is a tactic to frustrate the Brexit process and pursue their main objective of stopping it all together.

Labour leader Jeremy Corbyn reaches out to other party leaders and opposition MPs with a letter on 14 August 2019 asking them to support him as a 'caretaker Prime Minister' to block a no-deal scenario. The Conservative minority Government can be unseated if other parties form a coalition with Corbyn as leader.

Corbyn writes, 'Following a successful vote of no confidence in the Government, I would then, as Leader of the Opposition, seek the confidence of the House for a strictly time-limited, temporary Government with the aim of calling a general election, and securing the necessary extensions of Article 50. In that general election, Labour will be committed to a public vote on the terms of leaving the European Union, including an option to Remain.'

Corbyn's letter is sent to: Ian Blackford, SNP Leader; Jo Swinson, Leader of the Lib-Dems; Liz Saville Roberts, Plaid Cymru Leader; Caroline Lucas MP; Dominic Grieve MP; Sir Oliver Letwin MP; Nick Boles MP; and Caroline Spelman MP. The letter fails to specify the length of a 'time-limited' government and He doesn't get much support, but it doesn't fall on deaf ears either.

Jo Swinson (Lib-Dems) is up for the plot but is not convinced that Corbyn could bring the other parties together. She suggests Conservative MP Kenneth Clarke for the caretaker role.

It would definitely be considered a treacherous act if Conservative MPs overthrow 'a genuine government of unity' to install 'a Labour government supported by other parties'. Conservative Remainer MPs Sir Oliver Letwin, Dominic Grieve, and Caroline Spelman only agree to meet to discuss the different ways parties might work together to avoid no-deal.

In an interview Corbyn says, 'A caretaker government should be led by Labour... We, the Labour Party, by far the largest opposition party, have, I think, a responsibility to take over, to ensure there is no cliff-edge Brexit.'

Nicholas Boles MP, a Remainer, had resigned his (Con) party whip in April 2019 because his party refused to compromise on Brexit. His bill, the Common Market 2.0 proposal, failed at 261-282 votes. Despite the Chief Whip declaring it a 'free vote', the whips had successfully persuaded MPs to abstain.

Boles replies to Corbyn's letter, highlighting four issues that are dividing MPs opposed to a no-deal Brexit. This is a direct response to Corbyn's attempt to halt the 'chaos and dislocation of Boris Johnson's no-deal Brexit'.

Boles writes, 'I do not believe that this proposal is workable.

I, for one, will not support a vote of no confidence while the Johnson Government continues to pursue a Brexit deal that might deliver an orderly exit from the EU. Nor would I be able to support any government in which you were prime minister, however temporary its mandate.'

'Several other MPs sitting on the Opposition benches have said the same. I therefore urge you and the leaders of the other opposition parties to focus on legislative measures to stop a no-deal Brexit on 31 October.'

Boles goes on to say in no uncertain terms that the only way to succeed is to frustrate Johnson's plans.

Corbyn fails to get enough support for his plot, leaving the cross-party alliance of MPs in disarray.

Sir Oliver Letwin says in a BBC radio interview, 'I don't think it's at all likely that a majority would be formed for (Corbyn's proposal), and I personally wouldn't want to vote for it. I wouldn't be able to support that, no. ... You can't just say, "I don't want to have a no-deal exit" – you also have to say, "what do I want to have" and get agreement on that.'

Does Boris have a mandate for a no-deal Brexit?

Philip Hammond (Ind), Guto Bebb (Con), and David Gauke (Ind) all say, 'There's no mandate for a no-deal Brexit.'
Let's analyse the referendum question:

'Should the United Kingdom remain a member of the European Union or leave the European Union?'

It is a question without conditions. It does not say 'remain on newly negotiated terms' or 'leave with a deal'. A negotiated deal to leave is a conditional deal that contravenes the answer to the question on the ballot. The Government clearly has a mandate for a no-deal Brexit.

August 2019 - Johnson asks the Queen to prorogue

Summer recess begins on Thursday 25 July and the next sitting of the House is on Tuesday 3 September 2019 at 2:30 pm. Despite the 'crisis' MPs are talking about, they certainly don't want to miss their five weeks of well-deserved holiday. If Labour want to table a vote of no confidence to kick off Corbyn's coup then it has to be done now. Due to a lack of support Corbyn decides not to go through with it.
So, five weeks later....

Parliamentarians are refreshed and raring to go. After all, the country is in a bit of a pickle, about to crash out of the EU, go over a cliff edge and into the abyss. One might even say, it's an existential crisis and time one pulled one's finger out.

So, back to work on 3 September, just in time for the House of Commons to declare a recess again for the annual party conference season, which normally starts mid-September. This year the annual party conference recess is planned from 13 September to 8 October 2019. Conferences are booked a year in advance and there's no return of your deposit on the venue if there's a no show. Keynote speakers aren't paid but those who attend pay for their tickets, so it's an important event to raise funds for party coffers, and for the whole membership to be involved in policy making.

Parliament takes a conference recess every year

As a comparison, the party conference recess in 2018 started from 13 September to 9 October, in 2017 party conferences where held from 14 September to 9 October.

Which party conferences took place?

All the party conferences took place in 2019. MPs voted successfully to only block the recess to stop the Tory Party conference. The political parties have always agreed not to have Parliamentary sittings during this time so that they could all attend their respective conferences.

14-17 Sept. 2019 - Lib-Dems in Bournemouth, England

20-21 September - UKIP in Caerleon, Wales

21-25 September 2019 - Labour in Brighton, England

4-6 October - Green Party in Newport, Wales.

13-15 October – SNP in Aberdeen, Scotland

Parliamentary sessions normally last one year. Due to the Brexit crisis, the current session has been ongoing since 13 June 2017. They have been in session for over two years.

As the newly elected Prime Minister, Johnson claims he needs time to hammer out plans for the country's future and prepare his legislative agenda for the opening of a new Parliament in October he wants to prorogue Parliament.

On 28 August 2019, Johnson asks Queen Elizabeth II to prorogue parliament between 9 and 12 September. This amounts to just four days before the conference recess.

The Queen gives her consent

An interview with Sir John Redwood MP (Con) and Layla Moran MP (Lib-Dems) on 28 August highlights the difference in opinions during this time. Moran says proroguing is to avoid scrutiny of Johnson's Brexit plans. After a five-week holiday, she emphatically says they should cancel all party conferences to sit in Parliament and debate Brexit (no party ever considered cancelling their party conference).

Redwood says, 'We are following precedent, we always have three weeks off for the party conferences and then we usually have a short gap at the end of each parliamentary year, now the previous government decides to go for the biggest ever, long session, it is high time we had a new Queen's Speech and a full debate about the direction of the Government with a new prime minister. I'm looking forward to that Queen's Speech and I would recommend Opposition MPs join in that debate.'

Moran replies, 'I WANT TO WORK. It is utterly ridiculous that at a time of crisis, if you were in any other job and your organization was going through a crisis, let alone the country, us, as parliamentarians should be able to do our jobs, you're absolutely right, five weeks, Parliament has never been prorogued for five weeks before. And actually, I would argue why on earth would we have a conference recess at this time.'

The compère cuts her off with, 'But we have the conference season anyway.'

Moran replies, 'Well we shouldn't.'

(Once again, the Lib-Dems and all other parties have never even considered cancelling a conference!)

Compère, 'But we have the conference season anyway, I mean, you've got four fewer days to do the business that you want to do than you would have done without this, surely if you get your act together you can do the things you want to do.'

Moran, 'People are scared, and no-deal Brexit has real consequences, particularly for the most vulnerable, we're talking about food shortages, medicine shortages, this is the Government that has said this, the same Government that is proroguing us. ... Boris Johnson is basically a coward; he doesn't want to face us parliamentarians, he is stopping the people through their representatives from having their voice and this must be stopped, and it will be stopped.'

Compère, 'And if Prime Minister Jeremy Corbyn can stop a no-deal are you OK with that?' (refering to Corbyn's coup!)

Moran, 'We, everyone, is pulling together to make sure that no-deal will not happen.'

I must admit, Johnson never struck me as someone to shy away from conflict. The worst thing of all during this time is how MPs behave. They make the public believe that there has never been a recess during September/October. The behaviour of Remain MPs is tantamount to inciting a riot creating an angry response from the public to a mere four-day extension to the annual party conference season.

Jeremy Corbyn and Liberal Democrat leader Jo Swinson demand an intervention from the Queen. She declines.

3 September 2019 - First day after summer recess

Back from their five-weeks of holiday and MPs are up in arms about losing four days in Parliament.

THE BOTTOM LINE

If it's so important to debate Brexit in Parliament, why has no MP tabled a motion to shorten the five-weeks vacation?

Jeremy Corbyn's plot to thwart a 'no-deal' Brexit starts on Tuesday (3 September), Sir Oliver Letwin (Con) tables a motion to take control of the parliamentary agenda on Wednesday. The House of Commons passes Letwin's motion by 328 votes in favour to 301 against, a majority of 27.

Corbyn says: 'Suspending Parliament is not acceptable, it is not on. What the prime minister is doing is a smash and grab on our democracy to force through a no-deal.'

Philip Hammond leads 21 Tory 'Remain' MPs in defying a three-line whip to help vote down the motion – they lose the whip for abstaining. The rebel's include nine former high-ranking Cabinet ministers, like Ken Clarke. The irony is that, with a majority of 27, the motion will pass whether they vote or not. This kamikaze action by 21 Tory MPs achieves nothing except losing them the whip and getting them sacked. The sacking of 21 MPs is not a decision taken lightly as the Conservatives now have only 305 seats, this leaves them 21 short of a majority, which requires 326 seats.

Boris confirms that the sacking was necessary as you can't have your own MPs handing over the power of Government to the Opposition.

Phillip Lee (Con) defects to the Lib-Dems by walking across the floor to join them in a symbolic act of protest.

4 September 2019 - Second day after summer recess

MPs in a cross-party alliance, take control of the agenda in the House and pass a bill to force an extension if MPs do not approve the deal stopping a no-deal Brexit.

Johnson warns that he will seek an early election if MPs rule out a no-deal Brexit. Labour Leader Corbyn replies that he will only agree to an election when a no-deal Brexit is ruled out. Corbyn's stance has support from the other parties.

Johnson takes his first PMQs since announcing the prorogation of Parliament, after which Hilary Benn's 'Benn bill', is debated. This is the European Union (Withdrawal) (No. 2) bill, dubbed by Johnson as the 'surrender bill' because he believes it takes away any leverage from the UK's negotiating position with the EU. It passes on its third reading in the House of Commons, 327 votes to 299.

Johnson's motion for a snap election is voted down by 298 - 65. Johnson makes his famous remark, 'I would rather be "dead in a ditch" than ask the EU for a further Brexit delay.'

6 September 2019 - Benn bill passed by Lords

In closing the debate, Brexit Minister Lord Martin Callanan says, 'the "Benn" Act undermines the Government's efforts to negotiate a withdrawal agreement.' The legislation is presented for Royal Assent and becomes law on 9 September.

MPs continue to disrespect the will of the people

Boris Johnson is fighting an up hill struggle with his own party which is firmly in the hands of 'Remainers' who are determined to frustrate the Brexit process. These are the same Conservative MPs who sabotaged every effort by Theresa May to move Brexit forward. The question is, will Johnson suffer the same fate?

Johnson must weed out those treacherous MPs defying the will of the people.

9 September 2019 - Parliament is prorogued

John Bercow, who has been Speaker of the House since June 2009, announces his resignation. He will leave his post before the House resumes after the next general election. He doesn't receive a knighthood for his services to the Country.

PM Johnson makes one last attempt to get support for a general election by tabling a motion. With 293 votes in favour, 46 against, and 303 abstaining, it fails to get the two-thirds majority of 434 votes Johnson needs.

Parliament is prorogued just before 02:00 BST on the morning of Wednesday 10 September, to reopen on 14 October. The Conservatives leave the House; other parties stay behind as a protest against Johnson's action.

Let the court cases begin

Gina Miller, backed by former PM John Major, loses a bid to reverse Johnson's decision to prorogue Parliament for five weeks. The Lord Chief Justice, Lord Burnett, says, ,We have concluded that, whilst we should grant permission to apply for judicial review, the claim must be dismissed.'

Miller's claim that Johnson's advice to the Queen is an ,unlawful abuse of power' is confirmed by the Supreme Court. Their ruling in her favour states, 'It did not need to look at the motive of prorogation, but that what mattered was the effect of prorogation.'

The Supreme Court reached its judgement unanimously on 24 September and found that proroguing for five weeks was unlawful. Parliament is to resume on 25 September 2019. This is right in the middle of the party conference season.

Separately, the Court of Session in Edinburgh rules that Johnson's Parliament shutdown is unlawful. However, this ruling has no consequences as Scottish courts have no jurisdiction over the UK Parliament.

In the meantime, the Lib-Dems, UKIP, and Labour are enjoying their party conferences - until the news comes in that they must return to Westminster on 25 September at 11:30 am. Boris Johnson is attending the UN General Assembly in New York at the time and must cut his visit short.

25 September 2019 - Day 1 after court ruling

John Bercow addresses the returned MPs, 'Colleagues, welcome back to our place of work. The UK Supreme Court ruled yesterday that Parliament has not been prorogued and that the Speaker of the House of Commons and the Lords' Speaker can take immediate steps to enable each house to meet as soon as possible to decide upon a way forward.'

The Attorney General, the Rt Hon Geoffrey Cox, gives a statement on the prorogation of Parliament and takes questions from MPs justifying the Government's position.

Boris Johnson asks Corbyn to call the general election that he'd agreed to once the Benn Act became law. Why won't he do this? He invites Corbyn to call a motion of no confidence to trigger an election. Corbyn deflects and declines to do so. No legislation is made this Wednesday, just a lot of ranting.

26 September 2019 - Day 2 - Not much done today

John Bercow begins by reprimanding MPs for their dreadful behaviour in the House the previous day, 'There was an atmosphere in the chamber worse than any I've known in my 22 years in the House. On both sides, passions were inflamed, angry words were uttered, the culture was toxic.'

A motion is tabled to adjourn parliament for one week to allow Tory politicians to attend their party conference in Manchester. It is voted down by 306 votes to 289. Eight Tory MPs have the whip removed for voting against the motion.

MPs' hue and cry over previous weeks about their right to debate in Parliament during this time of crisis is already losing momentum. By 4:00 pm, fewer than 50 MPs out of a possible 650 are attending debates. Obviously, enthusiasm is waning by day two. Steve Baker (Con) talks to a near-empty House about the similarities between the abandoned EU Constitution Treaty and the Lisbon Treaty.

The whole thing becomes a bit of a joke as there is really no agenda due to it being party conference season. It's obvious that MPs only wanted to do political damage to Johnson and slow down the Brexit process to weaken his position.

29 September - 2 October - Tory party conference

Conservatives get-together under the motto 'Get Brexit Done'.

3 October 2019 - Parliament negotiation update

Boris updates Parliament on the current state of play in the negotiations with the EU. He announces the replacement of the backstop, preventing a hard border between Northern Ireland and the Republic of Ireland. After which, once again MPs speak to a near-empty house.

I thought Layla Moran MP and her Lib-Dem colleagues were eager to get back to work? Alas, as with previous Parliamentary sessions this week, they left with the others and are nowhere to be seen.

14 October 2019 - Queen's Speech opens Parliament

17 October 2019 - 'We have a deal'

When the EU Commission President Jean-Claude Juncker announces that 'We have a deal' there should be a sigh of relief among all MPs back in Blighty as all that effort to avoid a no-deal has paid off because 'We have a deal!'.

Boris calls it a great new deal that takes back control. Even before anyone has seen it, the deal is immediately rejected by Arlene Foster, Leader of the DUP, and by the Labour leader Jeremy Corbyn.

19 October 2019 - Super Saturday - the House votes

The actual substance of Johnson's deal is not much different from Theresa May's deal, which was turned down by Parliament three times. The main change is the way Northern Ireland's border with Ireland is dealt with. It allows Northern Ireland to remain part of the UK, and the free movement of goods into Ireland. Some MPs are already claiming that it is worse than the old deal. Worse being a relative term, because a deal that might be acceptable to the House of Commons has got to be a worse deal in the eyes of Remainers.

To kick the day off, Sir Oliver Letwin (Ind) - one of the 21 Conservative MPs who lost the whip back in September - tables the 'Letwin Amendment', which passes by 322 votes to 306. This amendment ties Johnson's hands and forces him to request an extension via the Benn Act regardless of whether Parliament votes the deal through this day or not. This has got to be one of the cleverest smash and grabs on our democracy to frustrate a bill that I have seen.

The European Union (Withdrawal) Act 2018 makes ratification of any deal dependent upon prior enactment of another Act of Parliament to approve the final terms of the deal. Approval for Boris Johnson's deal is withheld until Parliament passes the necessary law to enact the agreement.

The Government is forced to cancel the main vote, which was to approve the deal. Scheduling a 'meaningful vote' on the Withdrawal Agreement bill (WAB) for the following Tuesday (22 October). With now only 297 Conservative MPs, the numbers of the minority government are dwindling because so many have either left or had the whip withdrawn.

Boris reluctantly requests Article 50 extension

A letter requesting an extension for Article 50 to 31 January 2020 is sent to Tusk, as required by the Benn Act. A second letter from Boris to Tusk explains the events of the day and his commitment to seek ratification of the deal next week.

Corbyn's war cry - Deal threatens workers' rights

The withdrawal deal is only concerned with three points, as we've already discussed. Workers' rights are certainly not one of those points. That is a matter for Parliament to decide post Brexit and is certainly nothing to do with leaving the EU. True, there are EU regulations that cover workers' rights, and I would expect any future Labour party to ensure those rights are protected, but to suggest that it should be part of a withdrawal agreement is simply making trouble unnecessarily. According to the Withdrawal Agreement, EU legislation will be carried over into UK law. The reason being, there is so much of it, picking it apart to weed out the bits that nobody likes will take the next 40 years.

21 October 2019 - Speaker refuses vote on WAB

22 October 2019 - WAB passed by the House

The Withdrawal Agreement Bill passes its second reading in the House with 329 votes in favour, 299 against. As MPs turned down a fast-track timetable of just three days to debate it 322 votes to 308, Johnson pauses the WAB.

This is a monumental moment, as it was at this stage Theresa May's deal failed; on the other hand only a fast-track timetable will achieve an exit by 31 October, as promised by Boris Johnson.

28 October 2019 – EU grant flextension

The third extension to Brexit, to 31 January 2020, is accepted by the EU27. If the WAB is accepted by Parliament then the UK can exit with a deal at the beginning of any month before this date. Boris calls for a general election to happen on 12 December 2019 under the Fixed-term Parliaments Act, which requires 434 votes in order to pass. But so many MPs abstain he gets just 299 votes in favour and 70 against, the motion fails.

29 October 2019 - What a difference a day makes

The Lib-Dems and SNP, now state that they will back an election on 9 December, Boris tables a bill calling for an election on the 12 December 2019. This bill only needs a simple majority to pass. However, it is open to amendments, which could complicate matters as the SNP want the voting age lowered to 16 and for EU citizens to be allowed the vote. Both amendments are flatly rejected by the Speaker of the House. In a surprise move, Corbyn gives a morning interview in support of an immediate election without conditions.

The bill calling for an election passes, 438 to 20. This is more than the two-thirds majority that is required by the Fixed-term Parliaments Act and is the same bill that failed only yesterday. Why this bill passed? The power of the whip!

The political parties go into campaign mode. The late Cilla Black might have summed it up like this:

'Well chuck, there's candidate one (Boris) who'd rather be dead in a ditch than spend a minute longer with the ex. No ifs, no buts, he's out the door, with or without a deal.'

'Then there's candidate two (Corbyn) whose been a Eurosceptic all his life, bless his little cotton socks. He now wants to renegotiate Brexit, hold a second referendum so he can campaign against the very deal he's negotiated and remain in the club.'

'Well, what can I say, candidate three's (Swinson) gorra lorra, lorra, lorra nerve wanting to withdraw Article 50 with no referendum at all and move on like nothing ever happened.'

'Candidate four (Farage) is like a spring coil waiting to be released on the public.'

The decision is yours...

MPs are distraught that the election will be fought chiefly on Brexit and not the wider issues the country is facing. Labour and the Lib-Dems run campaigns on other issues, but this is without doubt a Brexit election.

12 Dec. 2019 – A landslide victory for Boris Johnson

The BBC is so shaken by the result that they underplay it, describing it as a 'sizable win for the Conservatives'. It took them a full three days before they used the word 'landslide'. Boris Johnson now presides over an 80-seat majority in the House. The Labour Party suffers the biggest defeat of all time as the Conservatives actually win seats that had only ever been Labour held. This is a clear message from the people to their Government. (Can this be considered a 2nd referendum?).
... Strike Six!

The 2016 referendum delivered a clear mandate to Parliament. Those MPs who didn't listen to the people and did everything in their power to frustrate the will of the people are now voted out. The 2019 election cleared out those MPs who refused to act on behalf of their constituents seeing 140 MPs lose their seats and being replaced.

Boris Johnson now has a clear mandate from the people and a majority in Parliament allowing him to get Brexit done.

DEMOCRACY HAS
FINALLY BEEN RESTORED.

The following maps compare the 2016 referendum result with how people voted in the 2019 election.

As mentioned earlier, if the referendum was tallied on a constituency basis, as elections are calculated, then the Leave result was overwhelming. Comparing the maps shows how this translated into electoral votes in 2019.

People were at their whits end with the disgraceful behaviour of Parliament in recent months and wanted their voices heard. The fact that Sedgefield (Tony Blair had a 25,000 voter majority here), Workington, Darlington and other 'red wall' Labour heartland constituencies in the north, who had never strayed from Labour, now voted for Boris Johnson!

Despite winning a House majority of 80 seats, his party betrays him three years later ousting him even after winning a vote of no confidence. Yet again the treachery and skulduggery from a handful of politicians disrespectful of the democratic process driving their own agenda. Is it coincidence that Liz Truss, a Remainer takes the helm just as important negotiations concerning Brexit are coming to a head?

31 January 2020 – Britain exits the EU

The countdown to 11:00 pm (GMT) on 31 January 2020 marks the end of an era and the beginning of negotiations for Britain's future relationship with the EU.

HOW CONSTITUENCIES VOTED IN THE 2016 REFERENDUM

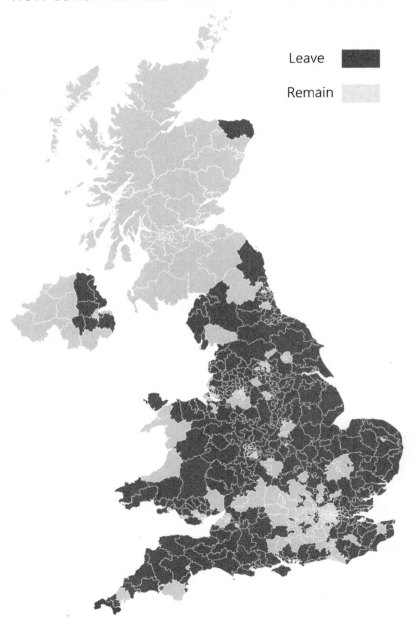

HOW CONSTITUENCIES VOTED IN THE 2019 ELECTION

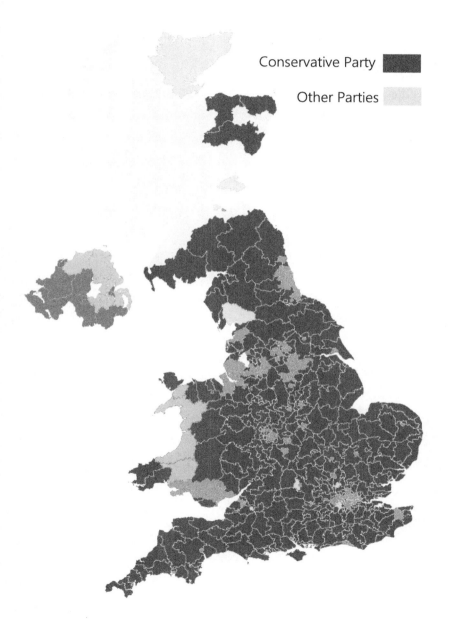

Conservative Party

Other Parties

THE EPILOGUE

The EU started out as a way to make wars' between neighbouring nations within Europe unthinkable, with the ultimate goal of creating a United States of Europe.

The Common Market, formed during the Thatcher years, brought European countries closer together as trading partners. The introduction of a single currency created the eurozone binding them even closer and seeing the beginning of real dependence on one another.

In principle, a United States of Europe sounds like a good idea. Take the USA for example which started with a blank canvas. There was no transport infrastructure, no bridges, no rule of law ... they were building a nation from scratch. It made sense to implement a single currency and have a federal Government that could step in when disaster loomed.

The situation in Europe is different. Is it wise to dismantle mature well-functioning institutions and replace them with a suprastate. Cultural differences within Europe can be extreme, but it is those differences that make Europe work. As Thatcher said, let the Spanish be Spanish, and the French be French.

The facts laid out in this book will certainly make you better informed and I hope have opened your eyes to some of the events that took place between Britain and the EU.

Was Brexit inevitable?

During Britain's 47 years of membership, pro-European leaders could never talk about remaining in the EU without including the word 'reform'. None of them were really happy.

If only Britain had helped form EU policies from the beginning and had not been blocked twice by the French, only to join 16 years late, it might have been a different story.

Sir Geoffrey Howe highlights this point in his famous resignation speech November 1990, 'If we had been in from the start, as almost everybody now acknowledges, we should have had more, not less, influence over the Europe in which we live today.'

**Every single prime minister since 1973,
without exception talked about EU reforms.**

Prime Minister Harold Wilson said just before the first referendum, 'We felt the terms (of the EEC) were grossly inadequate, many vital interests had been given away. We said we would renegotiate and at the end of that process we would ask the British people to decide.'

Declassified documents published by the National Archives give an insight as to how Margaret Thatcher felt about the Common Fisheries Policy. In September 1979 she wrote:

'The fisheries situation was already sufficiently unsatisfactory without our making further concessions. The so-called reciprocity of historic sights was meaningless since the French had fished out their own waters and British access to those waters was worthless.'

The 1983 Labour Party manifesto calls for leaving the EEC without a referendum. Tony Blair tells voters; 'We'll negotiate withdrawal from the EEC, which has drained our natural resources and destroyed jobs.'

The CAP rebate, fought for by Prime Minister Margaret Thatcher June 1984 and her famous Bruges speech September 1988 were all attempts to facilitate reform. Thatcher said, 'If we cannot reform those Community policies which are patently wrong or ineffective and which are rightly causing public disquiet, then we shall not get the public support for the Community's future development.'

Labour's 1997 winning manifesto said a lot about EU reform. Tony Blair's May 1997 Labour Manifesto speech, 'Europe isn't working in the way this country and Europe need... We have set out a detailed agenda for reform... Urgent reform of the Common Agricultural Policy (CAP). It is costly, vulnerable to fraud and not geared to environmental protection'.

September 2011 - Some 80 Conservative MPs form the European Conservatives and Reformists (ECR) party, whose aim is to discuss steps leading to EU reform.

David Cameron said in November 2011, 'Europe is heading in

the wrong direction without any chance of reform...'. David Cameron spoke for more than three years about EU reform during his time in office.

EC President Jose Manuel Barroso, September 2012 'A deal that combines the need to keep our social market economies on one hand and the need to reform them on the other.'

David Cameron, June 2015 – 'The European Union needs to change. Britain's relationship with the European Union needs to change, and I've got a plan to achieve that: reform, renegotiation, and referendum.'

And there are so many more examples...

With the exception of Margaret Thatcher's CAP rebate, no real reforms or compromises were ever made by the EU during Britain's 47 years of membership.

Brexit Undone?

Since Brexit day; 31 January 2020, there have been further attempts by Parliament and the media to hijack democracy.

Boris Johnson, voted in as prime minister with an 80 seat majority should have only stepped down as leader if voters demanded it. The handful of Tory MPs who resigned after Johnson had just won a vote of confidence, hijacked democracy forcing Johnson's hand to resign his leadership position. Was it really about eating cake on his Birthday or was there something more sinister motivating these treacherous

MPs? To no-ones surprise, Boris was replaced by a Remainer!

Post-Brexit, the British media blamed Boris for the shortage of lorry drivers, the cost of living crisis, increases in taxes. A ruthless political witch-hunt ensued that put him in a corner.

Comparisons can certainly be drawn with the ousting of Margaret Thatcher from the Conservative Party in November 1990. Thatcher was against signing the Maastricht Treaty, later calling it a treaty too far. Ousted by her own Party and replaced by John Major who went on to sign it, before being voted into the job by the people. This wasn't the first time such tactics have been employed. Gordon Brown, wasn't voted into his leadership position by the people and signed the Lisbon Treaty.

The replacement prime minister Liz Truss was a Lib-Dem up to 1995 and voted 'Remain' during the 2016 Referendum. Just after becoming prime minister she commented that she wants to change the things that are holding Britain back. An ominous statement to make, don't you think?

Within the first few weeks in power, she has demonstrated that she is hardly capable of running a country and the press are already talking about Boris running in the next election.

It seems that the Brexit saga is still not over...

Hotlifestyle.info

 Paulmcqueen.co.uk

Printed in Great Britain
by Amazon

19664353R00163